Using Literacy to Develop Thinking Skills with Children Aged 7-11

Ce
L
P
P

Related titles of interest

Using Literacy to Develop Thinking Skills with Children Aged 5–7
Paula Iley
1–84312–282–0

Teaching Thinking Skills Across the Primary Curriculum
A practical approach for all abilities
Belle Wallace (ed.)
1–85346–766–9

Teaching Thinking Skills Across the Middle Years
A practical approach for children aged 9–14
Belle Wallace and Richard Bentley (eds)
1–85346–767–7

Thinking Skills and Problem-solving – an Inclusive Approach
A practical guide for teachers in primary schools
Belle Wallace, June Maker, Diana Cave and Simon Chandler
1–84312–107–7

Using History to Develop Thinking Skills at Key Stage 2
Belle Wallace and Peter Riches
1–85346–928–9

Using Science to Develop Thinking Skills at Key Stage 1
Practical resources for gifted and talented learners
Max de Boo
1–84312–150–6

Discovering and Developing Talent in Schools
An Inclusive Approach
Bette Gray-Fow
1–84312–669–9

Challenges in Primary Science
Meeting the Needs of Able Young Scientists at Key Stage 2
David Coates and Helen Wilson
1–84312–013–5

Gifted and Talented Education from A–Z
Jacquie Buttriss and Ann Callander
1–84312–256–1

Think About It!
Thinking Skills Activities for Years 3 and 4
Jacquie Buttriss and Ann Callander
1–84312–234–0

Using Literacy to Develop Thinking Skills with Children Aged 7–11

Paula Iley

David Fulton Publishers

In association with
The National Association for Able Children in Education

I should very much like to thank the children and staff, past and present, of Grove C of E Primary School, Wantage, Oxfordshire and Kineton C of E Primary School, Kineton, Warwickshire in particular for their contributions to this book. Gratitude is also due to all the other schools and classes in which I have worked over the years, whose teachers and pupils have enabled me to trial and refine the ideas contained here.

David Fulton Publishers Ltd
The Chiswick Centre, 414 Chiswick High Road, London W4 5TF

www.fultonpublishers.co.uk

First published in Great Britain in 2005 by David Fulton Publishers.

10 9 8 7 6 5 4 3 2 1

Note: The right of Paula Iley to be identified as the author of this work has been asserted by her in accordance with the Copyright, Designs and Patents Act 1988.

Copyright © Paula Iley 2005

British Library Cataloguing in Publication Data
A catalogue record for this book is available from the British Library.

David Fulton Publishers is a division of ITV plc.

ISBN 1 84312 283 9

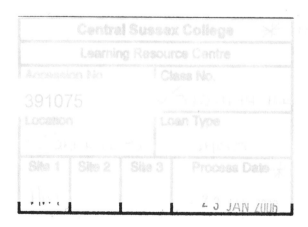
Typeset by RefineCatch Limited, Bungay, Suffolk
Printed and bound in Great Britain

Contents

Each of the three chapters is organised into six sections:

1 Problem-solving
2 Creative-solving
3 Critical thinking
4 Affective thinking and Emotional literacy
5 Questioning skills
6 Case study

NACE Membership

National Association
for Able Children
in Education

NACE exists solely to support the daily work of teacher providing for pupils with high abilities whilst enabling all pupils to flourish.

We are a large association of professionals offering a wealth of experience in working with more able pupils. We provide advice, training and materials on learning and teaching; leadership and management; whole school improvement; to schools and local authorities.

We provide:

- Specialist advice and information
- The Challenge Award. A Self-Evaluation Framework for Schools & LAs
- Professional Development Courses with optional online continuing support
- Bespoke courses and guidance delivered at your premises
- Tutors to work alongside teachers in the classroom
- Major Annual and Regional Conferences
- Market-leading books for teachers
- Exciting, challenging books for able children
- Keynote speakers for special events
- Support for special projects

NACE membership gives you:

- Quick access to professional advice and resources
- Members' website
- Termly newsletters and journal articles
- Discount on courses, national conferences and seminars
- Discount on The Challenge Award Framework
- Discount on The Challenge Award Subscription Documents
- Access to a national network of members and regional groups

Founded in 1984, NACE membership includes schools, corporate bodies and individuals. Members are teachers, headteachers, school coordinators, education advisers and officers, Ofsted inspectors, psychologist, researchers, HMI university and college staff, school governors, parents and educators from overseas.

Nationally NACE has regular contact with DfES, QCA, ACCAC, Ofsted, TTA, BECTA, London Gifted & Talented and the National Academy for Gifted and Talented Youth. Internationally NACE is affiliated to the European Council for High Ability and the World Council for Gifted and Talented Children.

In Partnership with Granada Learning Professional Development, David Fulton Publishers and Rising Stars UK Ltd

Visit - w w w . n a c e . c o . u k

or call us on - 0 1 8 6 5   8 6 1 8 7 9

Registered Charity No: 327230 - VAT No: 536 5807 26

NACE
P O Box 242
Arnolds Way
Oxford
OX2 9FR

T: **+44 (0) 1865 861879**
F: +44 (0) 1865 861880
E: info@nace.co.uk
W: www.nace.co.uk

Designed by Rooks Move Ltd - info@rooksmove.co.uk – 0845 2300 525

ADVANCING TEACHING : INSPIRING ABLE LEARNERS EVERY DAY

Introduction

In literacy lessons and beyond, children think a lot. So do teachers and the other adults around them. But is the thinking truly shared out? Are pupils learning to think independently, or are adults doing much of the 'thinking work' for them? Moreover, where, in our schools, is most value placed: on the product (the role-play performed, the text read, the writing completed) or on the process – what is being learnt along the way? Sometimes children assume that they have not 'worked' until there is something concrete to show for it; yet it is often in the 'stream of doing', which may precede or even supplant this end (and thinking is surely a powerful kind of doing) that learners evolve at all.

Thinking happens in any literacy-based activity. A group discussion demands that pupils reason with, and reflect on, others' views; a text being read cannot be passively absorbed, but requires 'decoding', and ought to be questioned and engaged with; and any writing task is full of choices to be made and problems to be solved. Effective teachers can plan for different degrees of challenge in these thought processes. But we need to ask ourselves, are the pupils aware of their responsibility for these processes, or do they see themselves as mere receivers of learning (in which case, a dependency culture flourishes)?

Some teaching approaches described here will be familiar. However, this book's main aim transcends the specifics of lessons and activities: it tries to give teachers a framework for drawing out the thinking skills lurking in literacy lessons. Its organisation helps teachers to *name* the types of thinking children are using (in terms they can grasp – see pages 5–6 for suggestions). Teachers should talk about thinking *explicitly* with pupils, thus enabling them to understand their learning and, ultimately, to manage it better. (For reasons of space I urge explicit discussion here in the Introduction, and not beside every activity the book outlines, as I should have preferred!)

So what types of thinking are there?

Gardner (1993, 2000, 2001, and subsequently) suggests that people have different kinds of 'intelligence' – visual/spatial, linguistic, mathematical/logical, interpersonal (social), intrapersonal (self-sufficient), musical, physical, naturalistic, spiritual/existential – and that one or more of these predominates in all learners. The suggestion behind the theory is that individuals may favour thinking and learning in nine (or more) distinctive ways, corresponding to these types. However, learning environments such as classrooms often prohibit such multifarious and rigid differentiations of task amongst a group; moreover, surely learners should become as 'rounded' as they can be, in which case pupils notable for their 'physical intelligence' should, arguably, gain experience of 'mathematical/logical' thinking, 'intrapersonal' learners of 'interpersonal' thinking, and so on. Similarly, ongoing research into right- and left-brain thinking, and different learning styles (VAK: visual, auditory and kinaesthetic), can perhaps mislead us into narrow, exclusive practices when teaching, and may ultimately be unhelpful in suggesting a framework for teaching thinking skills.

Most writers distinguish thinking from intelligence, as well as from knowledge: de Bono (1976), for instance, believes that thinking – other than daydreaming – is the process of 'achieving a desired mental state or result'. **Bloom** (1956), in his taxonomy of educational objectives (see Figure I.1), suggests a hierarchy that distinguishes between low-level, medium-level and high-level thinking skills. Note that recall, knowledge and understanding, which may predominate in school planning documents, are skills which Bloom considers low-level, and positions at the bottom of his hierarchy! Though they are important, he believes it is what the learner *does* with them that counts.

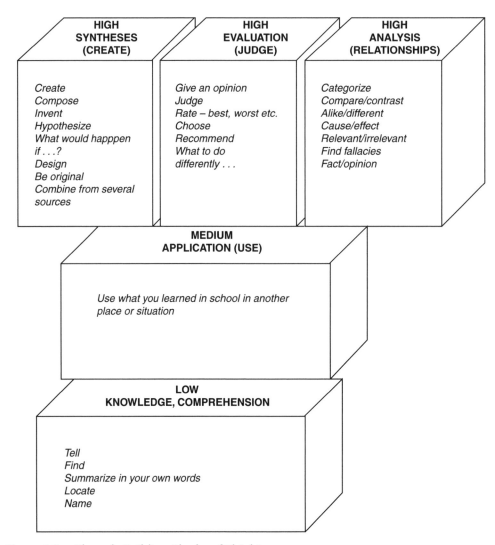

Figure I.1 Bloom's Building Blocks of Thinking

Source: From Benjamin S. Bloom, *Taxonomy of Educational Objectives*. Published by Allyn and Bacon, Boston, MA. Copyright © 1956 by Pearson Education. Adapted by permission of the publisher

Bloom gives the higher-level thinking skills of analysis, synthesis and evaluation a hierarchy too: analysis lowest, evaluation highest; in Figure I.1 here, following other writers on the subject, I do not. I do however, with others, see metacognition (thinking about one's thinking and learning), which Bloom considers an evaluative skill, to be perhaps the most challenging type of thinking that there is. Note that each set of skills, in its separate 'building block', is not discrete: during a learning experience, children may apply thinking from more than one 'set', or teachers may design an activity by combining ideas drawn from one 'set' with ideas drawn from another. Unlike Bloom, educationalists these days do not believe that a learner must progress chronologically 'from the bottom' in their thinking skills towards some 'top', but rather, fluidly 'moves' from skill to skill as the need arises; nonetheless, his overall categorisation is helpful.

The framework for this book also draws on **Fisher** (1990, 1995, 2003). Apart from his considerable work on philosophy for children, for which, sadly, there is no room in these pages, he describes at least three important types of thinking skill: critical, creative and problem-solving. Loosely, his notion of critical thinking is synonymous with Bloom's of evaluation (although Fisher also includes analysis in this 'skill set'); his notion of creative thinking corresponds roughly to Bloom's of synthesis.

'Problem-solving' as such is a term unused by Bloom, but it is present in much thinking skills-related literature (and is sometimes termed 'investigative thinking'). Examining Bloom's model, problem-solving seems to me to correspond to two of his skill sets combined, namely analysis *and* application: to solve a problem surely the learner must first analyse it, i.e. work out how its parts relate to the whole, etc.; thereafter s/he can set about tackling it. Bloom does not convince me that the latter process is a lower-level skill: it involves selectiveness, discrimination, calculation of risk, versatility, adaptability and more.

Both Bloom and Fisher suggest a key difference between creative thinking and problem-solving. Creative thinking is often 'thinking outside the box', or 'lateral thinking'. It is divergent, wide-ranging and not directed to one particular end: a metaphor might be the searchlight, roaming everywhere and anywhere, to my mind unjudgemental and far-seeing (though Fisher (1990) adds the critical dimension, valuing only 'creative solutions' that are also 'better solutions'). Problem-solving, I would argue, is in many ways the opposite: convergent, applied and directed to an intended goal. The more open or varied the choices (e.g. of resources or methods to use), the more creative the thinking required; the more limited, the more problem-solving the task. It is almost impossible when problem-solving to refrain from critical thinking at the same time, as the learner may often find themselves questioning whether what s/he is doing is effective and of value. The metaphor for both problem-solving and critical thinking might be a laser, probing and unravelling the detail. All three thinking modes seem to me invaluable. Sometimes learners may adopt two or three in the course of one task, other times predominantly one. In my view, all have their uses: none is superior.

Belle **Wallace's** TASC wheel (2000, see Figure I.2) is intended to help children establish 'where they are' in the thinking and learning process at any stage of a task or block of work. (During some lesson sequences, learners may just follow some

Figure I.2   My TASC problem-solving wheel

Source: © Belle Wallace, 2000, *Teaching the Very Able Child*, David Fulton
Publishers

phases on the wheel, or follow them slightly out of sequence; indeed, lessons may become too inflexible and homogeneous if the phases are slavishly followed as shown.) Although it is often described as a problem-solving diagram, the wheel encompasses all three thinking modes, as I have outlined them. Gathering knowledge is a divergent activity, i.e. it entails creative thinking, while organising it can require problem-solving; identifying the task needs analytical skill again, i.e. problem-solving; generating ideas calls once more for divergent, creative thinking; deciding on an effective approach necessitates critical thinking and problem-solving; implementing it *is* problem-solving; evaluating work done calls on critical thinking; communicating the work may require both problem-solving and creative thinking, depending on the scope for choice; and considering what has been learnt is Bloom's highest-level critical thinking, or metacognition.

However, there are other sets of thinking skills, beside the three already mentioned. **De Bono** (1970, 1976, 2000) divides thinking into six kinds, each signalled and encouraged in the classroom with the learner's donning of an appropriately coloured hat®:

- factual thinking (white);
- subjective thoughts and feelings (red);
- critical, logical thinking (black);
- positive, optimistic thinking (yellow);
- new thinking: alternatives, etc. (green); and
- thinking about thinking: metacognition (blue).

Some of these modes have already been covered by the three types outlined earlier; others, for example factual and logical thinking (termed by some 'reasoning skills' and 'information processing'), I suggest can be seen as part of problem-solving, at least in the context of literacy. I have therefore chosen to subsume them into that category.

Another skill set listed by many, sometimes called 'enquiry skills', is surely important enough to warrant separate treatment in this book – indeed, it is arguably one of the most crucial skill sets to tackle. Fisher (2003) and others, stress that the development of truly independent thinking skills requires the ethos of a *community of enquiry* in the classroom. Only by fostering high-level questioning skills in children, in literacy *and* across the curriculum, can teachers realistically hope to rebalance any culture of adults over-controlling over-dependent pupils, of knowledge and 'content' overwhelming skills, and the aim of some end-product dominating the continual learning process.

There is another dimension to thinking skills underplayed in most curricula for Western students. **Krathwohl** *et al.* (1965) argued that beside Bloom's cognitive, rational taxonomy published in 1956 lay an alternative, 'affective' taxonomy, based (in summary) on the degree of learners' commitment to their learning. Gardner (1993, 2000, 2001), too, as we have seen, suggests that there are learners with notable intrapersonal 'intelligences', i.e. strong powers of introspection and self-sufficiency; de Bono (1970, 1976, 2000) also promotes the importance of voicing subjective thoughts and feelings, and of optimistic thinking; Fisher sees 'affective strategies', i.e. the ability to think independently of others while taking their views into account, as a key aspect of critical thinking; while other writers list 'affective qualities', including 'learning stamina', versatility, adaptability and resourcefulness.

Currently, much is also being written about 'emotional intelligence' or 'emotional literacy': the ability to explore one's own thoughts and feelings (which coincides somewhat with the notion of metacognition, already mentioned); to empathise with the feelings and situations of others; and to help, mediate and lead, socialise and collaborate with others in a variety of settings and roles. Such ideas chime with Gardner's notion of 'interpersonal intelligence'.

This book has three chapters – Speaking and Listening, Reading and Writing – covering literacy opportunities in English lessons and across the curriculum. Within these I have therefore created the following sections:

- Problem-solving (covering both analysis *and* application to tasks: with younger children you might call these aspects 'working out what we are looking at' and 'sorting things out').

- Creative thinking (you might describe this as 'opening up our minds to lots of ideas').

- Critical thinking (you could call this 'deciding what we think'). For simplicity, I have suggested approaches here that stand alone, or that can begin or end literacy tasks, rather than approaches interwoven with the other kinds of thinking listed.

- Questioning skills.

- Affective thinking and emotional literacy (you might explain these as 'thinking about people's feelings', or 'getting on by ourselves', 'with ourselves' or 'with others', depending on the task).

- Case studies: sequences of lessons described in more detail; they incorporate several of the 'skill sets' above in a three-stage format of 'plan-do-review'. This format is versatile and rich in thinking possibilities, and resembles that advocated by Wallace (2000) in her TASC wheel, and other writers such as **Eyre** (1997).

You or your school might use the five headings listed above (excluding 'plan-do-review') to audit the extent to which these thinking-skill sets are currently addressed in your planning documentation, whether just in literacy or more widely. You can then perhaps begin to redress any imbalances by injecting more 'thinking-based' activities similar to those that this book suggests.

Most approaches described in the pages that follow are deliberately general, often listing examples merely of how they might be applied to different 'literacy content'. This is intended to encourage teachers to try the ideas in as wide a variety of contexts as they can. Nearly all the activities are accompanied by suggestions on differentiation. However, beware: a thinking-skills approach to the curriculum often surprises teachers in terms of what children can achieve!

To illustrate this, below are some checklists of the behaviours of able language users. It is rare to find able learners who exhibit all of these, all the time, in every context. With this proviso, they may be useful in your school or classroom to aid identification. Note that they are generic, not age- or 'literacy-level'-related; indeed, many bullet points describe ways of thinking and 'casts of mind'. In using them to observe children, you may find yourself looking anew at learners you already know, for the effect of considering their thinking skills in any area of the curriculum is that these skills often transcend, and sometimes contradict, children's officially recognised achievements, uncovering their nascent potential instead.

Able speakers and listeners *may*:

- Show enthusiasm for, and stamina when, speaking: say more; talk about complex ideas; embroider talk with relevant illustrations, reasons or anecdotes . . .

- Get absorbed in listening or show pronounced listening behaviours: ask pertinent questions; recall accurately and in detail; build elaborately or thoughtfully on the speech of others . . .

- Use and enjoy using the metalanguage (technical terminology) of speaking and listening: 'dialogue', 'pause', 'gesture', 'interrupt', etc.

- Choose and control their speaking behaviours independently: organise their utterances appropriately; manage complex ideas or complex sentences; invite others to contribute; choose imaginative wording and phrasing; sustain an appropriate tone, register or volume; engage and sustain listeners' attention . . .

- Choose and control their listening behaviours independently: ask appropriate or insightful questions at appropriate times; produce considered responses; involve several speakers or listeners in discussion by mediating; record listening, e.g. in note form, succinctly and successfully; use responsive body language . . .

- Choose types of speaking and listening appropriate to a task, observing the 'rules' of the type chosen.

- Choose types of speaking and listening adventurously for themselves, being prepared to take risks: improvisation, interview, impersonation, unusual vocal effects, etc.

- Show emotional maturity in relation to issues, themes and the 'politics' of speaking and listening.

- Be self-aware as speakers and listeners, knowing their preferences, strengths and weaknesses.

- Be self-critical, and able and willing to improve their speaking and listening skills.

Able readers *may*:

- Be enthusiastic about their reading and enjoy discussing it.

- Use and enjoy using the metalanguage of texts: 'alliteration', 'paragraph', 'italics', 'traditional tale', etc.

- Be capable of immersing themselves in texts, and of showing stamina, e.g. with challenging or 'alien' texts.

- Independently go beyond 'decoding' to take an active approach when reading, e.g.:

  - using inference and deduction (inferential skills)

  - hypothesising

  - recognising or accepting ambiguity or uncertainty, or

  - interrogating the author/text, e.g. their purpose.

- Be capable independently of seeing a 'big picture' in relation to texts, e.g.:

  - giving a detailed view supported by evidence or examples

  - collating ideas or information from several places in texts, or several texts

  - seeing the larger 'shapes' and intentions of texts

  - comparing/contrasting texts/aspects of texts, or

  - drawing on their own life experience to respond to texts.

- Empathise with points of view other than their own, e.g. the author's, a character's.

- Show emotional maturity in relation to issues and themes raised by texts.

- Be self-aware as readers, knowing their preferences, reading habits, strengths and weaknesses.

- Be self-critical, and able and willing to improve their reading, e.g. by trying unknown texts, reading strategies and techniques.

Able writers *may*:

- Be enthusiastic about their writing and enjoy discussing it.

- Use and enjoy using the metalanguage of writing: 'comma', 'layout', 'scene-setting', etc.

- Apply their reading experiences readily to their writing.

- Independently manipulate and control the audiences and purposes of their writing to good effect.

- Independently control different aspects of their writing at the same time (orchestration), even when writing at length, e.g. the organisation and layout of a text, its punctuation *and* its spelling.

- Show a love of language and an adventurousness with vocabulary and phrasing in their texts.

- Independently make appropriate choices of text forms, types, styles and approaches, observing the 'rules' of the text/approach chosen.

- Be self-aware as writers, knowing their preferences, strengths and weaknesses.

- Be self-critical, and able and willing to improve their writing by revising and proofreading.

Note that able language users may not show all these behaviours, or show them in every learning context.

Paula Iley, 2005

CHAPTER 1

Speaking and listening

Problem-solving

Speaking *is* problem-solving: speakers have to decide what to say, how to say it and, while doing so, how to respond to their environment and other speakers. Listening is also problem-solving: listeners must make sense of auditory information and, often, decide how to respond – sometimes at speed. The following activities help heighten children's awareness of the analytical, decision-making and 'puzzle-solving' aspects of speaking and listening.

Sorting ideas

The following sub-sections describe several kinds of sorting to highlight during oracy activities.

Sequencing . . .

● . . . in preparation for talk

If recall is involved, for example, when individual children or groups are about to give instructions to someone, or recount or review actual events, choices of sequence may be limited, but they are still essential. (Sequencing becomes a 'puzzle', to be 'solved'.) If possible, ensure photographs or other images are available of anything actually experienced by the children. These illustrations can be imported on to an interactive board, stuck to a large board or provided to children in a set. Ensure they are in random order, and invite the children, individually or in groups/pairs, to sequence them from memory in preparation for their 'talk task', for example by dragging them around an interactive board, or sticking them on to card (a 'storyboard').

Speaking on a subject, or about an interest or hobby, does not often require *chronological* recall; however, speakers must still make decisions on a suitable order. Therefore, a collection of pictures or 'props' arranged into various 'sub-topics' also aids them (for instance, maps of different countries, personal logbooks, examples of coins and photographs of sites, if they wish to talk about coin collecting).

Speakers' chosen sequences should help guide the organisation of their talks.

● . . . during talk

If children are recounting real events, reviewing a text, TV programme or performance, or issuing instructions, invite them to devise 'speaking frames' for use while talking. They might like to write these up, e.g. on a display board, for easy reference when speaking. For example, a recount might start 'The first thing that happened was . . .', 'It was interesting when . . .', 'Shortly after that . . .', and proceed using frames such as 'By [time], . . .', 'Later, . . .' and 'One highlight was . . .'

Categorising

When children are listening, suggest that they 'group' (i.e. categorise) what they hear in some way, for example:

● From a play about an issue such as bullying, to group the characters according to their attitudes.

● From a programme or interview about a subject, for instance food and cooking, to categorise things talked about, e.g. into food groups.

● During a group discussion about an object or 'product', to 'batch together' the various comments about it according to degrees of approval or criticism.

● From dramatised or recorded dialogue in which speech varies widely, to sort quotations based on degrees of formality, accent, language used, etc.

- From several role-played examples or videoed clips of talks, to label them as types, e.g. discussion, interview, monologue, conversation, drama, etc.

Making choices

Allow speakers some scope for choice, for instance, to:

- speak *either* about a favourite read *or* a favourite film;
- present a subject they have researched *either* to a younger class *or* to an older class;
- show and explain *either* an object *or* a picture connected with a subject studied;
- *either* explain how they made something *or* how they did something (e.g. a game or activity undertaken);
- retell *either* a known story, *or* something that happened to them recently;
- do a group presentation *either* about a shared piece of work *or* of a shared interest;
- interview a hotseated speaker in role as one of two choices of character/person;
- read aloud *either* a prayer poem *or* an epitaph poem;
- give instructions for a task involving *either* equipment that is currently out of reach *or* action by several people (e.g. a game);
- designate *either* a chairperson and a scribe in a group *or* a chairperson and a spokesperson;
- *either* write notes *or* draw a concept map in order to record ideas or findings in a group/pair; or
- make/do something *either* in one 'challenging' group/pair *or* in another.

How can you manage?

Limiting children's 'speaking and listening resources' can present them with thought-provoking challenges. For instance:

- Ask them to describe a process, e.g. an experiment or model-making, without the 'prop/s'.

- When they are making up their own stories to tell, stipulate one story setting only, of the speaker's choice.

- Similarly, stipulate two or three characters maximum when they are story-telling.

- Challenge them to describe a person or object without using certain words, e.g. an Egyptian mummy without using the words 'bandage', 'linen' and 'preserve'; their audience must guess the subject.

- Insist they give instructions without touching or indicating essential equipment/materials, and without demonstrating any of the procedures.

- While listening to a talk, video or TV programme, forbid children to respond verbally, with instant questions or reactions. Instead, invite them to memorise or record questions for later on.

- Forbid 'negative' utterances during group discussion/interaction, e.g. sentences beginning 'But', 'No', 'That's not fair', 'Stop', etc.

- Confine each member of a group to fulfilling one role, e.g. chairperson, scribe, doer/maker, talk monitor (checking that the group uses the 'target language', e.g. of negotiation) or spokesperson (watching the task and reporting back).

- Give the less dominant member of a 'talk pair' the crucial role, e.g. reader, writer, doer or spokesperson (watching the task and reporting back).

- Give group discussion/interaction tasks a time limit.

- Alternatively, constrain resources, e.g. allocate one pencil, page, glossary or thesaurus per group when recording or researching a subject.

- As a drama challenge, ask children to enact a scenario using only 'gibberish' words, e.g. an angry mother and repentant daughter.

In all cases, encourage children to think *why* you are imposing these constraints; explain the benefits.

DIFFERENTIATION

In a mixed-ability group, some children will benefit from such constraints, some may not; this will not necessarily depend on ability.

Finding shapes, finding patterns

The notion of 'shape' describes the distinctive way in which a listening experience may be organised and sequenced, for example a talk may enumerate several stages of an activity, in chronological order, and a TV programme may begin and end with the same 'tag-line'. The notion of 'pattern' describes any form of repetition, e.g. the rhyme scheme in a recited poem; a recurring question, never answered, in a recorded interview; or a frequent catchphrase in a story being told. Of course, speakers and other 'sound producers' (performance poets, broadcasters, etc.)

also 'break' patterns – sometimes intentionally, for effect. The following two categories of activity heighten children's awareness of such features. They are most successful if children listen to the talk/performance several times: the first time for general enjoyment and understanding.

Mapping and tracking

- If children are listening to an account of a journey (on TV, recorded or 'live'), for instance in RE, history or geography, provide them beforehand with a pictorial map of locations mentioned. (For confident listeners, ensure the map includes places *not* mentioned in the account: aural 'red herrings'.) While listening, ask the children to number places mentioned in the order they are referred to. Afterwards, they can 'join up the dots' to indicate the route described.

- If children are listening to an account of events or changes over time, e.g. an historical account or a scientific process, supply them beforehand with a time-line. (For confident listeners, ensure the line includes times *not* mentioned: aural 'red herrings'.) While listening, ask the children to check off the times mentioned.

- During any group discussion/interaction where you have asked for an eventual consensus, designate one child per group as 'talk monitor'. Ask them to record in some way the process of reaching agreement, e.g. initial notes on the sequence of individual contributions, followed by a diagram to represent the 'journey', with all its 'ebbs and flows', towards agreement.

DIFFERENTIATION

Ask confident listeners to listen for more features, uncertain listeners for fewer. Get the latter to work with partners who concentrate well.

Comparing and contrasting

- Choose a group discussion in which the ideas of group members are being pooled, for instance tips for cyclists' road safety, or what children already know about the Tudors. Designate one child per group as 'talk monitor', asking them to observe the contributions of group members. Afterwards, ask them to report which peers agreed or made similar contributions, and which disagreed or made original contributions.

- Use a listening context in which several things or people are described, for example a programme about soluble and insoluble solids. Ask listeners to spot as many differences and similarities as they can, for example, in the appearance and forms of different solids, their behaviour in water and their degrees of likeness to liquids.

- After any listening experience in which events are recounted, e.g. a play, story, biographical or autobiographical account, present children with a list of some events. Ask them to distinguish major incidents from minor ones. Encourage debate; children must justify their views.

DIFFERENTIATION

Able listeners participating in any comparing/contrasting activity can be challenged to listen only once; uncertain listeners may benefit from listening again (if possible record any talk, dramatic scene or reading so that you can replay it). They will also need shorter listening experiences. Alternatively, interrupt their listening at regular intervals, questioning them to ensure that they are 'still on listening task'.

Solving puzzles, using clues

There are puzzles in much of what we listen to: some with definite 'answers', some without.

Information gap

Be alert to listening contexts in which 'information gaps' are there for children to explore. For instance, it may be possible to ask:

- How did the character/s feel? (If feelings were betrayed only by actions or speech.)

- Why did the character/s behave, or events happen, as they did?

- Who is/was it? (If an action was described without attributing it to one character.)

- How did the character/s do that? (If a problem or solution was narrated without a detailed explanation of how.)

- What could be the title of that piece?

Ask children to justify their answers. Some 'puzzles' will be open to a variety of ideas. For instance, having heard a rendition of the traditional ballad 'The Twa Corbies', or its variant 'The Three Ravens', children can speculate widely about who the 'slain knight' is, how he might have died, who might have killed him and why.

Many cross-curricular puzzle-solving opportunities can be created through listening to informative videos and TV programmes. For example, having watched a recorded programme about the features of a choice of sites for an ancient settlement in Britain, children can decide, in groups, which site a population should have selected and why. Then view the rest of the recording to check their conclusions.

Another kind of puzzle is presented when listening to a text whose language is not readily accessible, for example a recorded extract from Chaucer's *Canterbury Tales*, a play by Shakespeare or a poem in an unfamiliar dialect. Ask children to follow a copy of the text, and perhaps refer to some helpful illustrations, while listening; afterwards ask them, in pairs or groups, to attempt a translation, using their inferential skills to guess obscure words and phrases.

> ## DIFFERENTIATION
>
> Leave your questioning open for confident 'listening detectives'; give the unsure children a finite choice of 'answers' to your questioning. For example, they might listen to a reading of Sharon Creech's diary-poem *Love that Dog*; afterwards, if you are asking the class why the boy refuses to write a poem about a pet, give the less confident three possible answers written down: either he hated animals, or he didn't have a pet or he was still too upset about his own dog's death. Ask children to quote you the proof, where it is available, to justify their ideas.

Guessing games

- 'Turn down the sound' occasionally while children are listening to a recording, programme, talk or reading (the reader can mouth silently). Invite children to guess which words or phrases have been missed. They should tell you which words they heard just before and after the silence, to help justify their ideas. This is an especially useful approach with specialist vocabulary or knowledge; for instance you might hope children would volunteer, 'I knew the missing phrase was "upthrust and gravity" because the word before was "When" and the words after were "are equal or balanced, an object will float". They are the things that have to be equal for something to float.'

- Read or say two or three sentences and invite children to tell you where a new paragraph or punctuation mark should be, e.g. a comma, semi-colon or colon. They should 'race' to put their hands up at the appropriate moments (alternatively, they can raise 'new paragraph' or punctuation-mark cards). Ask them to suggest which words occur immediately before and after. Again, they must justify their answers – for instance, 'I knew the new paragraph started there because the next words are "He tossed and turned *that night*", so the time changed.'

> ## DIFFERENTIATION
>
> Get more able listeners to respond independently. Less confident listeners can share their ideas with a trusted 'talk partner' before suggesting their answer.

Exploring dilemmas

Many stories, real-life reminiscences, informative texts that describe different people's moral and cultural values, narrative poems and enacted dramas suggest difficult decision-making situations. Use contexts such as:

- a totally unexpected state of affairs, e.g. the hero's shock 'feminisation' at the beginning of a teacher-read or play version of *Bill's New Frock* by Anne Fine;

- a dangerous situation, e.g. the choice, in an audio-book extract from Joe Simpson's autobiographical *Touching the Void*, of whether one climber should save himself by cutting his rope;

- a religious dilemma, e.g. the description in an RE text of a Muslim schoolchild being required to do a lesson at prayer time on a Friday;

- conflict or an argument, e.g. one of many episodes from the *Tracey Beaker* TV series (based on the Jacqueline Wilson character);

- the problem of how much truth to tell, which might be the focus of a scenario used in school assembly; or

- the difficulty of saying sorry, e.g. as witnessed in a real classroom situation in which the teacher intervenes.

Draw the children's attention to the dilemma as it unfolds. Stop it before a solution is reached. Invite the children to explore it for themselves through discussion or role-play, considering what they would do and why.

After feedback, celebrate children's most thoughtful and appropriate ideas, for example by asking them to rehearse and re-enact a short scene in front of others, or to produce a leaflet of advice.

DIFFERENTIATION

Let able thinkers consider their dilemmas unaided; support unconfident thinkers by suggesting a few resolutions. Some should be feasible, some should not 'fit' the context, and some should be unworkable.

Setting puzzles and dilemmas

Challenge especially able speakers and listeners to set their own oral puzzles or dilemmas for peers to 'solve', as in the following two sub-sections.

Puzzles

- If children have a language or dialect unknown to some peers, ask them to improvise and polish a simple dramatised scene in that 'language', using plenty of props, gestures and physical action. They can then invite their audience to guess its gist.

- Ask them to find or write a short dramatic scene in which some information is not made explicit, e.g. a character's feelings or true identity. Again, they can act it out and ask their audience to guess the unstated information.

- If the class has been researching a subject, challenge them to set verbal clues about it for a peer group. For example, if they have found out who in class has the longest and shortest arm and leg bones, they can give clues as to their identity – details about the children's hobbies, family members, appearance, and so on. The children they challenge to solve such 'puzzles' must register the clues without recording them.

Dilemmas

For drama work, give children a choice of plays and/or scenes from stories. Ask them to select one that contains a notable dilemma (see pages 15–16 for ideas). Alternatively, ask them to brainstorm ideas about dilemmas that might occur if they had a particular set of values (during PSHE, citizenship or RE work). Invite them to improvise, rehearse and then perform their chosen scenario; to stop it at the point where the dilemma occurs; and then to direct their audience to explore it in a manner of their choosing (e.g. role-play, discussion, debate, conscience alley,* artwork, agony aunt/uncle column, notes, etc.): what would *they* do? Take feedback, share ideas and celebrate the most thoughtful in some recorded form.

Creative thinking

Making patterns, making shapes

This approach can help develop children's abilities to undertake individual or group talks, or tell stories, to an audience. The notions of 'pattern' and 'shape' will first of all need exploration with the children, for instance by listening to recorded talks to spot the 'patterns' and 'shapes' used by others (see the explanations in the sub-sections below). Thereafter, invite them to plan 'patterns' and 'shapes' into the talks they give. If their audience is other children, challenge that audience to spot these 'patterns' and 'shapes'.

Patterning

A talk or story can deliberately repeat a feature for effect – a 'pattern', for example, a word or phrase; a catchphrase; an assumed voice or tone; an image; a question or exclamation; a theme or idea; or a rhythm of speech.

Shaping

- Several parts of a talk may be distinctively organised, for example into clear sections, or with a surprise ending. While taking about a book read or a show seen,

---

* In conscience alley, two lines of children form a 'tunnel' down which a character walks; those on either side state the pros and cons of the dilemma.

children might 'shape' their presentation with 'One thing I liked was. . .', 'Another thing I enjoyed was . . .', 'But the best thing of all was . . .'; in reporting on a local survey they might cover many aspects of the local environment but return repeatedly to one key theme, e.g. litter or wildlife.

- The events of a story may be 'patterned', e.g. each might be a 'new version' of the one before, or else the different events of a story might happen in the same set-ting, over and over. Alternatively, a story might include a 'patterned' refrain such as 'Days passed', 'A month passed', and then 'This time a whole year passed'.

- If a group tells a story or makes a presentation, they might follow a particular sequence of turn-taking, i.e. creating a 'shape'.

DIFFERENTIATION

Give confident speakers a larger number of ideas from which to choose than unconfident speakers, e.g. limit the latter to *either* repeating a word or phrase, *or* organising their talk into clear sections so that the audience can hear when one has finished and the next begins.

Design your own . . .

If you wish a child or group to do a talk or presentation on a subject, suggest that they design a format for it. Urge them to try the unusual, and yet be informative. Ideas might include:

- role-play as if they are participants in a programme on TV, e.g. a commentator or presenter, an interviewer and interviewee, or a discussion panel;

- group role-play as if each member is a witness arguing a case, e.g. in court, or at a council meeting;

- a short play, acting out events or conveying facts;

- a series of illustrations, held up and explained;

- a demonstration, e.g. of a model or collection;

- a Powerpoint or interactive whiteboard presentation; or

- an interactive demonstration/presentation using volunteers from the audience to help them, e.g. handling equipment, or 'trying out' props or activities.

DIFFERENTIATION

Free choice may suit more adventurous children; with others, limit the options, for example to two from the above list. For those who find organisation difficult, help them plan and timetable their preparations, and monitor their progress closely.

Same text, different meanings

Ask children to find ways of reading the same text aloud to produce quite different effects each time. Some ideas are suggested in the following four sub-sections.

Stories with at least two interpretations

Individuals can read these first in one tone of voice, then another. For example, *The True Story of the 3 Little Pigs!*, by Jon Scieszka, can be made to sound like the account of an unfairly maligned wolf or a catalogue of unconvincing excuses.

Stories written from two or more viewpoints

Groups, pairs or individuals can read these aloud so that they sound more sympathetic first to one character then another – for instance Ruby and Garnet in an extract from Jacqueline Wilson's *Double Act*.

A non-fiction text with a viewpoint

Individuals can read these in two ways: first matter-of-factly, and then so that it exposes the point of view of the writer. Newspaper reports are suited to this activity if they have bias, for example tabloid articles on a controversial subject such as asylum seekers, or anti-royalist reports about the British monarchy. Advertisements written and presented to seem primarily informative are also suitable, for example the 'advertisement features' or 'special promotions' on cooking or fashion in magazines.

Texts in which parts can be allocated

Pairs or groups can perform several different renditions of a text not originally intended for performance, e.g. poetry or fiction (this is sometimes known as 'readers' theatre'). Invite them to consider taking different reading 'parts', e.g. a narrator and participants, and/or to read some sections chorally; using sound effects, percussion/music, silences, actions and/or gestures; and/or involving the audience, e.g. in any chorus or repeated phrases. As examples, four children can interpret Anthony Browne's *Voices in the Park* several times, in several contrasting styles; two can read an extract from Raymond Briggs's *The Man* (a two-way dialogue) more than once, giving different impressions of the two characters; a group can 'perform' W.H. Auden's poem 'Night Mail' in several ways; or a pair/ group can read Harold Munro's 'Overheard on a Saltmarsh', to create two or more very different effects.

DIFFERENTIATION

Invite more perceptive children to arrive at their own interpretations. With unconfident readers, stipulate in what way their performances should sound different, e.g. one sarcastic, the other pleading. Suggest and model vocal techniques, gestures, etc. to help unsure performers. In work within groups, ensure that each has a competent organiser.

Stage directions

This is a listening-based activity. Children may undertake it while and after:

- listening to a recorded text such as a story or poem, for example on a listening centre; or

- watching and listening to a performance, e.g. a reading, a short play, a piece of music, or drama or music on TV.

The children listening must be able simultaneously to read and follow copies of the text, script or score. (If it is a live performance, prime them with detailed descriptions of what they will be listening to.) Ask them in advance to devise a marking code or symbols for different techniques they may hear used, e.g. raised/lowered voices or high/low volume, repetition of phrases or sounds, different sound effects, pauses and silence, changes in speed, individual parts, parts where several people perform at once, etc. Then, while listening, ask children to annotate the text using their marking system. Celebrate the records of those who have made the widest and greatest variety of observations. Also praise those who designed the most efficient and distinctive methods of annotation.

DIFFERENTIATION

Encourage able thinkers to devise their own annotation systems, even inviting them to think of the features they wish to annotate. Provide the less confident with a coding system of your own.

Teaching shared talk

This activity is also useful for summative or formative assessment after a significant period of using, and discussing the etiquette of, collaborative talk in class.

Ask children, in groups or pairs, to find a way of showing what they have learnt so far about:

- leading groups;

- taking any other roles in groups/pairs, e.g. scribe, spokesperson;

- good ways of ensuring that everyone has their say and plays their part;

- ensuring that some children are not left out, or stay too quiet;

- ensuring that some children do not say too much, or try to run things when they shouldn't; and

- good ways of responding to others' contributions, even if they don't like or agree with them.

Challenge them to design a way of teaching what they have learnt to others, for example children in a younger class; alternatively they could role-play addressing imaginary children engaged in playground arguments or leaders of several countries discussing whether to go to war. You might give them optional formats, such as:

- a mini-lesson, teacher style;
- a role-played example of collaborative talk, perhaps with a commentator;
- a short scripted play illustrating key points;
- a Powerpoint or interactive whiteboard demonstration; or
- a cartoon-strip fable, voiced-over by the children.

> ## DIFFERENTIATION
>
> Give adventurous children free choice of format, listing the ideas above as examples only. Give less confident children fewer choices.

How many uses for . . .?

Give children, individually or in pairs, a small collection of objects, for example a coathanger, a doorknob, a drumstick, a tennis racket and a deflated ball. Allow them five or ten minutes to think, and then ask them to improvise as many uses as they can for each object. For instance, the deflated ball might remind them of an animal's ear, a large flower petal, a bowl for a picnic, etc. Children can use mime only, inviting their audience to guess what they have in mind. Alternatively, they can speak and employ sound effects, turning each improvisation into a short dramatic (and potentially humorous!) scene. A more challenging variant is to ask groups or pairs of children to include the multiple uses of one object, or of several objects, all within one crazy, fast-paced mini-saga!

> ## DIFFERENTIATION
>
> Put able performers together; put diffident performers with trusted peers.

The ways people talk

Two possible ways of allowing children to explore the diversity of talk are described in the sub-sections below.

Identifying a script

Give children, in groups, a range of plays and/or stories, in only *some* of which characters vary widely in their social status and relationships, i.e. including family, friends, strangers, adults, children, 'foreigners' and 'important people'. Brief children to identify the texts amongst those you have given them that would be most suited to show a wide range of types of talk if they were dramatised. From those identified, ask them to choose one. They must discuss and then explain to the rest of the class how, within that text, they could make each character's language distinctive if performed as a play. Alternatively, ask groups to jot down 'director's notes' for the dialogue of each character. These should record their ideas on how the words should be spoken or could be adapted to highlight characters' special qualities and relationships with others. For example:

- The children could include appropriate jargon in the dialogue of a character whose work or hobby is important to the story.

- They could give characters a dialect, if those characters live in one location.

- A 'foreign' character could use a dialect, an accent or a non-standard version of English.

- 'Important' characters could speak in full sentences only, use longer words than others, and avoid contractions (i.e. saying 'cannot', instead of 'can't') – in other words using a formal register.

- Friends and close family could use slang, contractions and short, sometimes unfinished utterances, and occasionally transgress the standard English rules of grammatical agreement (e.g. not saying 'we were', but 'we was') – except, perhaps, when speaking with 'important' characters.

Acting out a script

Give children a play (or a story that is easily adapted to one) that has potential for a wide variety of talk, as described above. Ask them to rehearse and dramatise it, finding ways of clearly demonstrating the variety suggested above.

Some examples of stories or plays suited to these activities are the many versions available of *The Pied Piper of Hamelin*; *Sir Gawain and the Green Knight*; *The Lambton Worm*; Alfred Lord Tennyson's poem 'The Lady of Shalott'; and Roald Dahl's *Matilda*.

DIFFERENTIATION

Challenge able thinkers about talk to consider as diverse a range of types of talk as possible, without using reference materials. For children who are unsure about the differences in talk, give them a helpful glossary of key terms, e.g. slang, jargon, dialect, standard English, non-standard English, formal and informal language. Ask them to identify characters in the text whose language might 'fit' each of these terms.

Critical thinking

Many of the activities described below can follow, or combine with, those described in the 'Problem-solving' and 'Creative thinking' sections of this chapter. Most can equally stand alone.

Rating

Immediately after a listening experience, or their participation in talk, ask children to identify and rate (for example as first, second and third):

- the 'best' events, characters, settings, facts, descriptions, arguments or sound effects from what they were listening to;

- the 'top' speakers, characters or participants, e.g. in a talk, group discussion, performance, TV programme or video;

- the 'best' or most memorable phrases, lines, sentences, speeches, suggestions, arguments or pieces of dialogue they heard or participated in during talk, a presentation, performance or video;

- the 'top' listening or speaking experiences recently encountered;

- the 'best', funniest, most unusual, exciting, frightening, etc. stories or poems read aloud to them; or

- their favourite kinds of listening or talk experience.

They can agree this 'ranking' through discussion in a group, or decide it individually. Ask them to justify their preferences.

In further variants of this task:

- Ask children to invent three titles for a performance, programme or video watched, or a reading listened to, whose original title you have concealed. Alternatively, ask them to give three possible titles to a piece of drama they have performed. Afterwards ask them to rank these as their first, second and third favourites and to justify why.

- Invite individuals to rate and discuss their own 'listening performances' during several recent listening experiences.

- Get individuals to rate and discuss the quality of their talk during several recent occasions when they spoke at length or took part in a group/pair interaction.

Otherwise, express this same task as a question: 'If you could "buy" only one *x*, which would it be?' Urge them to justify their selection.

DIFFERENTIATION

Invite adventurous thinkers, speakers or listeners to do one of the above using a criterion of their own, e.g. funniest, clearest, most boring, most frightening, hardest, most persuasive, most unusual, most surprising, most interesting, most upsetting, most embarrassing.

Polarities

After a listening experience, e.g. a debate, a presentation, a video or piece of drama, give the children a shuffled pack of cards, each bearing one word from the following pairs of value-judgement words:

- right/wrong;
- good/bad;
- agree/disagree;

- like/dislike;
- sensible/stupid;
- easy/difficult;
- strong/weak;
- clear/confusing;
- polite/rude;
- persuasive/unconvincing;
- true/false;
- objective/biased; and
- for/against.

You may need to ensure that certain meanings are understood, for example 'objective'. You may also wish to exclude some word cards, depending on the listening experience, for example, the last four pairs listed above are particularly appropriate when children have been listening to 'issues-laden' material.

Invite the children to pick a card at random; challenge them to make statements about *either* some aspect of their listening experience *or* their own 'listening performance'. They must use the word on the card they have chosen. (Some will prove hard to use, and will require ingenuity!) They must justify their statements; for instance, of a watched role-play, 'When Krishan pretended to get upset with Gemma, his shouting sounded unconvincing [target word] *because it started before she had told him the truth.*' They can also build on each other's ideas, for instance, 'I don't think, *like Josie does*, that Philip is wrong to say we should all have football time in the playground; I think she's biased [target word] by the fact that she hates football.'

DIFFERENTIATION

Challenge more able thinkers to incorporate 'their' words into statements without help. Give unconfident thinkers and listeners more guidance, such as 'Think of a reason you have just heard for [target word] picking up litter.'

Reviewing talk

Reviews can happen after children have given a talk or presentation, conducted an interview, issued instructions, taken part in pair or group discussion or undertaken a drama activity. Before they do this task, ask them to remain alert throughout as to how they are tackling it, in what order, and to their thoughts and feelings. Afterwards, ask some of them:

- to recount what they did, in what sequence (e.g. planned a scenario for a TV warning about strangers: improvised a meeting with an unknown adult, discussed how to improve it, rehearsed and wrote down dialogue, practised the role-play again to bring out the point of 'stranger danger' more clearly); and/or

- to describe to others the features of their speaking and/or listening, using the metalanguage (specialist terminology) of oracy as much as possible (e.g. improvisation, discussion, dialogue, script, role-play, rehearsals); and/or

- to reflect on how they reacted to the task; what they thought and felt while speaking and/or listening; what helped them with it; and their feelings and impressions when it was done; and/or

- to record the process in some way, e.g. as a labelled flow-chart, and/or to jot down their thoughts about it, for example in a learning journal. (In this case, you may need to model the process first by demonstrating entries about your personal speaking and listening.)

Getting children used to 'observing themselves at work' in this way, on a regular basis, heightens their powers of metacognition.

DIFFERENTIATION

Allow able thinkers to describe the processes and their thoughts independently, in their own fashion. Ask thinkers who struggle either/or questions, for example if they can't remember the details of the task instanced above, ask whether it was to develop a drama about a stranger kidnapping a child *or* to advertise the dangers of meeting strangers; whether they scripted the scenario first, *or* role-played it first; and which parts of the process made them feel shy *or* confident. Uncertain children, particularly children with recall problems, should summarise these processes *immediately* after they finish; you may need to give them shorter oracy tasks in the first place.

Evaluations

Below are three sub-categories of this approach.

Giving opinions

After any listening experience, ask children what they think of:

- that kind of experience generally;

- the way the speaker/s spoke (e.g. intonation, diction, expressiveness, pace, pitch);

- the language used by the speaker/s (e.g. their vocabulary, any dialect, accent, typical phraseology, formality of English, register, etc.);

- the most striking facts, descriptions or episodes from the experience; or

- their own listening performance.

Ask each child for a 'snap judgement' on this in one or two words initially (you may wish to jot their ideas down); then discuss the 'item', for instance two or three striking parts of an interview, in more depth; finally, invite them to revise their initial impressions (recording any changes). Praise listeners able to extend their first responses.

An alternative approach is to select one aspect listed above and to ask:

- 'Do/did you like it? Why?'
- 'Do/did you find it funny, interesting, surprising, unusual, difficult to follow, etc.? Why?'

Also, periodically ask them about themselves:

- What do they consider their strengths and weaknesses?
- What kinds of listening do they like and dislike?
- Where and how do they like listening, e.g. how seated (or standing)? socially or in a quiet place, for instance wearing headphones?
- What kinds of talk do they like and dislike?
- What kinds of audience do they find it easier and harder to talk with or to?

Jotting down their responses – or asking them to, for example in a learning journal – heightens their self-awareness (metacognition).

DIFFERENTIATION

Giving opinions is often a more challenging activity than judging, outlined below, and therefore especially suited to more able thinkers. If inviting opinions from uncertain children, give them a limited choice of responses; for example when asking them to evaluate two or three striking parts of an interview, invite them to choose between adjectives such as 'aggressive', 'dynamic', 'energetic', 'vivid', 'descriptive', 'hilarious', 'informative', 'startling', etc. Where listeners struggle to explain *why* they liked or disliked a listening experience or found it hard to understand, ask them instead to explain *what* they liked, disliked or found difficult.

Judging

After a listening experience of any kind (hearing a talk, a reading or audio-book, or a presentation, or watching drama, a TV programme or video, or a computer experience with sound), canvass children's judgements on whether:

- they would like to keep the experience in a small imaginary 'listening suitcase', or not;
- they liked or disliked it (and how much, e.g. on a scale of 1 to 5);
- they found it boring or entertaining/interesting (and how much, e.g. on a scale);
- it held any surprises;
- it made them want to hear more of the same or similar;
- they found it hard or easy to follow; and/or
- they were pleased with their own 'listening performance'.

Ask children for a show of hands for or against, or undertake a 'secret ballot' on pieces of paper. Welcome diverse responses. Over time, you may wish to build up a star rating system for listening experiences the class or group has enjoyed.

> ## DIFFERENTIATION
>
> Encourage children with a wealth of language to suggest words of different 'intensities', matched, say, to the numbers 1 to 5 in a scale; for instance, if inviting the class to judge the complexity of a listening experience, the most articulate might suggest terms in a spectrum from 'bland' to 'straightforward', to 'varied', 'complicated' and 'confusing'. If necessary, introduce them to suitable terms.

Critical talk friends

Your children may already have 'talk partnerships', i.e. pairings for oral work across the curriculum. It often works to partner twos who would not choose each other, avoiding both close friendships and 'difficult' combinations!

Ask suitable talk pairs to sit together for any task where you expect a 'spoken product', whether shared between them or from each as an individual, e.g. a theory, a plan, an account of an activity undertaken, a presentation, a review or critique, or a response to a listening experience such as a video. Designate one in each pair A, the other B. Invite As to express and develop their ideas first, and Bs to comment on them; at a signal from you, Bs can express their ideas and As can comment. (If you are happy for pairs to develop a shared spoken outcome, now ask them to reach agreement on its form: setting a time limit helps.)

At the same time, set criteria for partners to use when evaluating each other's ideas. Ideally, the most confident speakers and listeners should devise these for you. For instance:

- If individuals are preparing what to say about a talk they have just heard, you might pre-set as indicators of success (a) the quotation of three facts, examples, incidents or descriptions from the talk, (b) their opinions of each, e.g. why they found them interesting or unusual, and (c) at least one question they would like to ask the speaker, referring to something they said. Pairs can judge if partners have met these criteria.

- If pairs are deciding on a joint theory about, for example, whether differently weighted objects fall at the same speed, you might give as the criteria for an effective theory (a) the use of at least two specialist terms (e.g. 'gravity'), (b) at least one reason for their theory, and (c) at least one suggestion about how the theory could be tested. Partners can again self-judge against these criteria.

Display the criteria in some visual form, for example as a list that can be ticked off on an interactive board. Whether the pairs are commenting on each other's ideas or pooling them, praise those who use the criteria, advise each other sensitively, listen to their partners and adjust their thinking accordingly.

Ensure that plenty of individuals or pairs have time to share their spoken 'product' aloud with the wider group or class.

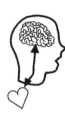

Affective thinking and emotional literacy

Tracking thoughts and feelings . . .

In Key Stage 1, your fellow teachers may well have drawn children's attention to the wide variety of human emotions: anger, fear, happiness, anxiety, surprise, like, dislike. . . . Teachers and children may have considered the differences in people's body language and behaviour when experiencing each feeling, and the kinds of situations that provoke them. Ideally, by Key Stage 2, children should be aware that no emotions are 'bad' – that all are valid, although they sometimes need to be managed and controlled.

You may, however, need to initiate or consolidate such work yourself. If so, begin by introducing a basic list of some of the most common emotions (such as those listed above). Work with children to devise corresponding emoticons (facial expression symbols intended to convey different feelings). These can be displayed, for instance on a classroom poster, and used not only in literacy but in many cross-curricular contexts.

Before undertaking some of the approaches outlined in the sub-sections below, KS2 children will need to be familiar with a wider, subtler range of emotions: introduce and discuss the meanings of such feelings as bravado, shyness, envy, jealousy, resentment, disappointment, disgust, apprehension, tension, diffidence, etc. Encourage children to spot and collect instances of these emotions from TV programmes, films and drama performances they watch, and audio-books and radio programmes they listen to. Again, a classroom display can be a useful teaching tool. Feature in it a selection of pictures and stills from radio and TV magazines and film and play reviews, labelled to explain the emotions conveyed by the protagonists in each, and the methods that they use to show them.

. . . through listening to fiction or recount

Undertake this activity having:

- watched and listened to a DVD, video or TV story or real-life recount, such as something historical, biographical or autobiographical;

- seen a group, class or school performance of fictional or actual events; or

- listened to a story, true or imagined.

Suitable accounts are those in which the feelings of one or more characters change, either explicitly or by inference.

- Ask children to record such fluctuations, using a set of class emoticons or some of their own devising. They can draw or stick these symbols in a sequence on a blank piece of paper, shadowing, as it were, the 'emotional shape' of the account.

- Provide children with digital photos, sketches or silhouettes of the protagonists at key moments, or sets of photocopies of these. Ask children to label each with 'feelings bubbles' (like thought bubbles), articulating the emotions they believe each protagonist felt at these points.

- Where thoughts *and* feelings are explored or implied, though not always clearly stated, ask children to label each protagonist with thought *and* feelings bubbles.

DIFFERENTIATION

Emotionally mature children should design their own emoticons. Mature thinkers will be more challenged by stories and accounts with protagonists notably unlike themselves – adults, fantastical characters, people from other cultures or times, personalities with problems outside the children's own experience, etc. Invite them to speculate on these more 'foreign' thoughts and emotions. Get sophisticated thinkers about feelings also to consider accounts in which characters deny or hide their emotions.

Using a set of class emoticons is most supportive. Let less certain listeners hear the account or watch the 'performance' in stages, if possible. Ask them to record the emotions of the characters as they occur. Thus they will still complete an overview of the whole 'emotional journey'. (Alternatively, ask the unconfident to record the emotions or speculate on the thoughts from one section of the 'listen', or of one character, only.)

After any such activity, encourage children to share and compare similar experiences and emotions they have known in their own lives.

. . . through drama about problems and relationships

Often, emotional and relationship issues preoccupy children. Many need sensitive handling, but common themes include:

- the absence of family members;
- bereavement and loss;
- teasing and bullying;
- fickle friendships;
- envy, copying and peer pressure;
- other forms of pressure, e.g. competition, school pressures;
- feeling left out or inferior;
- new siblings (or adults) in the home;
- rootlessness, displacement or disorientation;
- bias, prejudice, stereotyping and gender issues; and
- shyness and uncertainty.

These powerful subjects are often best tackled through the objectivity of drama. Improvisation and role-play can provide a safety net for difficult feelings, and can help develop children's thoughts in constructive ways by throwing up coping strategies and solutions. (Consult parents or carers fully in relation to some topics before beginning!)

Pick one or more of the themes above, as appropriate to children's needs. *Without* drawing attention to any relevant recent experiences, ask children, in small groups with trusted peers, to develop scenarios based on their allocated theme. During the drama, you can:

- ask the actors to 'freeze-frame' mid-dialogue or -action at key moments, and invite all – including the actors – to suggest out loud what the 'characters' might be thinking or feeling;

- give each child-spectator a small whiteboard with a think bubble drawn on it. At each freeze-framed moment, ask them to write in their bubbles what they guess one character is thinking or feeling;

- provide an enlarged image of the action at one or more key moments, e.g. on a classroom display board, showing each character in outline. Invite children to add think bubbles or captions to the display, speculating about how the characters were feeling (known as 'character in role').

Whatever the method chosen, give the children a chance to discuss their ideas carefully. This work can be completed by brainstorming a list of useful coping strategies and recording them in some form, e.g. as a poster for the wall, pamphlets for 'friendship monitors' in the playground, or advice stuck in home-school diaries.

DIFFERENTIATION

Challenge more capable speakers to invent their own scenarios. It may inspire children to show a suitable film clip or read a relevant text before beginning. Never insist all children participate: consult with them, and with their parents/ carers well in advance, if you are in any doubt whether to involve them. (Even observing such activities silently may help develop the thinking of children with relevant problems.) Give less confident actors a more closed brief, for example if asking them to enact a scene on the theme of prejudice, give them subject-matter for their dialogue, e.g. people who wear glasses.

. . . *through metacognition*

As in the 'Reviewing talk' approach in the 'Critical thinking' section of this chapter (pages 24–25), prime children to remain aware, when undertaking an individual or collaborative speaking task, of:

- what they thought and felt when they knew what they had to do;

- how their thoughts and feelings changed during the task; and

- their feelings and impressions when it was finished.

Give each speaker this list and ask them to jot down their responses during or immediately after the activity. Then get them to refine their observations in one of two ways:

1 Children should distinguish which of their observations were thoughts and which were feelings; for example, they might colour-code their notes into these two categories. (Ensure they are clear about the difference.)

2 Ask children to review their jottings orally, as if wearing *either* a red hat® (for their feelings and their thoughts) *or* a blue hat® (for their *thinking about* their feelings and thoughts). As an example, suppose you have asked groups to agree on a plan for a science experiment. Invited to review their impressions of the activity, one child might 'wear the red hat'® while reporting her recorded comment, 'I wrote down that I was worried about working in this group because I'm quite shy.' She might 'wear a blue hat'® to gloss this remark with, 'I keep trying to be less shy and I suppose this sort of work will help me if groups ask me nicely to say what I think, like they did today.'

DIFFERENTIATION

Both approaches described above are challenging, the second arguably more so. For children who find these hard, revert to the 'Reviewing talk' approach on pages 24–25.

Risk-taking

Openly discuss, and value with speakers and listeners, their ability and willingness to take risks; stress that risk-taking, i.e. trying unfamiliar things, is the only way learners learn. Challenge children sometimes to be 'brave enough' to make a choice or take a risk they would prefer not to. Some examples of speaking and listening that encourage risk-taking are:

- any listening experience with no preamble from the teacher explaining what it will be;

- working on an improvisation or role-play with a limited brief, e.g. simply a theme;

- a 'difficult listen' that requires intelligent guesses, e.g. about word meanings, or 'off-stage' events;

- a first-time speaking experience, e.g. a recital, a speaking part in a play, a presentation to a special visitor or a report in whole-school assembly;

- new demands while speaking or reading, e.g. to use new, specialist vocabulary, to give a talk using 'props' or to read aloud chorally;

- working with an unfamiliar or unchosen partner or group; and

- taking on a new role during group discussion and collaborative work, e.g. chairperson, reporter to the class, scribe, 'doer', instructor or 'talk monitor' (ensuring that the group is using the 'target language', e.g. the language of speculation, as modelled by the teacher).

Ideas from earlier sections

Many suggestions from earlier sections can contribute to affective thinking and emotional literacy, as shown under the sub-headings below.

Problem-solving

Allowing children to make at least some choices in their speaking and/or listening ('Making choices', page 11) empowers them, giving them a sense of ownership of their learning activity and often boosting their motivation, not to mention their self-esteem.

Under 'Exploring dilemmas' (pages 15–16), it is suggested that children should make 'real-life transference': give them the chance to share analogous experiences of their own, and to consider what they did, or would do, in similar situations. Dilemmas' (page 17) also allows them this opportunity.

Creative thinking

'Design your own . . .' (page 18) is another approach that empowers children by giving them scope for at least some choices.

The 'Same text, different meanings' approach (page 19) prompts children to see that there are many viewpoints in the world and to become aware of others' personalities and feelings.

'Teaching shared talk' (pages 20–21) encourages children's interpersonal skills, and their thinking about these skills, in the context of speaking and listening.

Asking children 'How many uses for . . .?' (page 21) encourages them to be flexible and wide-ranging in their thinking – a quality some term 'fluency'.

Critical thinking

The following approaches will help children become more aware of their interpersonal skills, and encourage them to reflect on areas for improvement:

- reviewing their speaking and listening during collaborative talk in groups and pairs (pages 24–25);
- 'Giving opinions' on their own speaking and listening preferences and performances (pages 25–26); and
- 'Critical talk friends' (page 27).

It should, however, be stressed that children also need opportunities to reflect on:

- Their capacity for working on some tasks *without* speaking to others ('intrapersonal' skills). Ask them when is this best, appropriate or useful? Praise and reward those who work silently and with concentration *in appropriate learning contexts*.

- Their strong preference for working silently and alone, where relevant. Ask them why is this not always practical, successful or helpful? What skills, understanding and knowledge can they learn best (or better) through talk? Praise and reward those who work collaboratively to great effect (using 'interpersonal' skills) *in appropriate learning contexts*.

Slotting approaches together

Many of the approaches described in 'Problem-solving', 'Creative thinking' and 'Critical thinking' – and in this section too – can be 'slotted together' to create an extended block of work if desired. Each phase should take children's thinking about their speaking and/or listening to a new level and help them develop 'learning stamina', one aspect of affective thinking.

Questioning skills

Always welcome appropriate questions, however inconvenient or mind-bending they may be! Stress – and ensure – that questioning is not the province of classroom adults alone. Discuss questioning, and emphasise its importance, openly; consider its difficulties honestly. Emphasise that it is only through curiosity and investigation that learners learn; explain that questioning enables children to play an active, rather than a passive, part in their learning, i.e. to help decide what they want and need to learn.

Formats and games

The formats and games in the following six sub-sections highlight oral questioning skills.

Interviews across the curriculum
Ask children to:

- interview tour guides, school visitors, subject experts and speakers;
- question people in the course of surveys;
- video conference, e.g. with subject experts; or
- interrogate adults or peers in role, e.g. through hotseating, or role-playing TV broadcasts, interviews or auditions.

Teacher statements
From time to time, use a single introductory statement to begin a new subject topic or to mark a new phase of activity within a unit of work, for example, 'We still don't know where the ancient Egyptians got their technology from', or 'Division in maths is hard.' Either make the statement orally, or write and display it clearly somewhere. Now invite the children's comments or questions in response, remaining silent except to act purely as 'chairperson' as their discussion continues. (If this is a new format, it may take children a while, and lots of encouragement, to get going!) Recording such responses can be fascinating and informative, providing detail that

is likely to aid the planning of future teaching as well as assessment. Don't be fooled: many remarks will probably be questions in disguise: 'I thought someone had found a lost city called Atlantis and Egyptian technology came from there', for example, would be a challenge to the teacher's wisdom and should be welcomed, while 'I can't remember what division is' would be a request for help, and should be acted on!

Barrier games

The teacher or a child conceals a picture or object, perhaps relevant to a subject being studied. One or more others then attempt to guess what it is, or to draw it, through dialogue and close questioning.

Who/what am I?

Sticker the foreheads of one or more children with a label stating who or what they are. They should try to guess the answer by questioning others. (Alternatively, children can be asked to write labels for each other.) This is a useful game for cross-curricular work if you confine subjects for labels to people, animals or things connected with a topic being studied.

Questions, questions, questions

Ask children, in pairs, to improvise dialogue as characters in a setting of their or your choosing. It must be conducted entirely in questions, e.g. 'Where are you going?', 'Why do you want to know?', 'Have you got something to hide?', 'What, this, you mean?', etc. Children who make statements, or who can't continue, are out.

Yes/no games

In 'Animal, vegetable or mineral?', 'Twenty questions' or other variants, invite a child to choose a plant, animal or thing connected with a subject topic. (Alternatively, they can choose an occupation, person or place.) Others must use questions that elicit only a 'Yes' or 'No' anwer, until they can guess what the chosen 'object' is.

DIFFERENTIATION

Debate, especially with able thinkers, which kinds of question are most difficult to form, and why. ('Why?' and 'How?' questions are hardest to formulate; they also tend to prompt a wider field of interesting, and longer, answers.) Challenge confident questioners to use an adjective or adverb with 'How?', e.g. 'How often?', 'How strong?', 'How soon?' Encourage them to probe the replies they receive, requesting more or clearer information or challenging the speaker, e.g. 'What do you mean?', 'Tell me more please', 'How do you know that?', 'But I thought you said . . .'.

Many KS1 classrooms display the whole group of so-called 'question words' so that children can use them interactively as prompts to aid question formulation. They are equally helpful in various KS2 settings: many older children still need practice devising interesting and appropriate questions beginning 'Who?', 'What?', 'When?' and 'Where?', as well as 'Why?' and 'How?' This word group steers weak questioners away from forms of enquiry that may otherwise often start with 'Do/Does?', or 'Is/Are?' (Such enquiries tend to 'close down' replies to 'Yes' or 'No'.)

Employ yes/no games to develop children's questioning skills once they are secure in using the group of question words above. These games challenge them to design their questions with ingenuity and an appropriate amount of detail, making them neither too vague and broad, nor too narrow and closed.

In pair games, encourage any children in the 'audience' to suggest appropriate questions. Record, display and celebrate especially good ones, taking class votes on them if desired. Suggest to struggling questioners one or two other key words beside the best 'question word', for example if a child is trying to ask a visiting author how she started writing, suggest 'How', 'first' and 'begin'.

Unfinished business

At the end of an activity, a unit of work or subject topic, ask children to volunteer questions they would still like answered around the theme. These responses should inform both your future planning and your assessment of the children's learning.

DIFFERENTIATION

Challenge able questioners to devise their own, original or interesting, question formats. Give less confident children speaking frames if needed: 'I would still like to know what/where/when/how/who/why/if/whether . . .', and 'Next time we study/do x, I wish I could/would like to/would rather . . .' (actually, these frames are 'questions in disguise'!).

PLAN-DO-REVIEW FORMATS: A CASE STUDY

The following example of a Speaking and Listening unit of work focused on Year 4 children's listening skills; it aimed to allow them to investigate how talk varies with age, familiarity and purpose. The activities developed problem-solving, creative and critical thinking skills, in particular. Lessons followed the useful and versatile sequence of 'plan-do-review', similar to that promoted by Belle Wallace in her TASC problem-solving wheel (see Introduction, page 4).

Differentiated objectives

As I had calculated, most intended learning outcomes suggested themselves to me as a result of the planning lesson described below.

Learning objectives (for the planning lesson): All children to be able to hear some distinguishing features of different types of talk on a tape played; some to be able to make useful notes on these while listening, and to hear the subtler distinctions, e.g. vocabulary and register, not just volume or speed; all to be able to suggest some ways of investigating differences in school-based talk (problem-solving); some to be able to suggest a variety of ways of carrying out the investigation (creative thinking), and/or the practical details of at least one investigation (problem-solving).

Learning objectives (from the 'doing' lessons): All children to be able to hear differences in talk, and to record them; some to be able to record them in note form; most to be able to distinguish these, e.g. different speeds, and place them in context, e.g. teacher–pupil or pupil–teacher (problem-solving); some to be able to categorise these within a context, i.e. various word differences such as slang spoken by children to each other (problem-solving).

Learning objectives (from the 'review' lesson): All children to be able to perceive that some features of talk, e.g. speed or volume, are common in certain situations; some children to be able to perceive that there is no 'correct' way of speaking but that some types of talk are more appropriate/practical in certain contexts (critical thinking).

Lesson one: planning (problem-solving and creative thinking)

I began with minimal preamble, announcing that I was about to play a tape and that the children's skills of listening and concentration would thus be tested. This home-made tape illustrated children and teachers talking in various contexts: lessons, the playground, dinnertime, travelling around school, in assembly, etc. (To sustain interest and concentration, I gave the 'fidgeters' worry beads to handle, or patterns on paper to colour in while listening; I also 'chunked' the experience by stopping the tape after each clip, challenging the children to identify the setting.)

   Next I wrote on the board 'Teachers and children talk in different ways. This depends on who and where they are.' I then invited the class to comment or raise queries on this theme, merely chairing the discussion with spurs such as 'Does anyone want to add to that/say something different?' The discussion took in not only school but home and other settings. As I had hoped, there was already some thinking about how talk might vary in different situations (the analytical side of problem-solving). Less aware listeners mentioned differences such as speed, volume and tone of talk (anger, humour, etc.). Some described other aspects: politeness, length of utterances, 'different words' and the fact that friends might speak differently from those with more distant or formal relationships (e.g. teacher and pupil): by doing so they were helpfully identifying themselves as the more acute listeners and analysts, perhaps capable of greater challenge in the lessons to follow.

   I recorded on the board some of the features of talk mentioned – volume, speed, tone and lengths of speech. I then replayed three clips, this time asking less aware listeners to notice and remember instances of the features I had listed. Meanwhile the rest were asked to record on paper, in two columns, examples of words that struck them as specific to speakers who knew each other well, or more formal talk such as in a lesson or assembly, teacher to pupil, or vice versa. I took feedback from various children afterwards, asking the note-takers for their thoughts based on their jottings. (One was struck by the 'bittiness' of children's utterances in situations of familiarity, as opposed to those longer, more complete utterances during teaching or assembly. Another noticed the slanginess and informality of language amongst children, e.g. 'Yeah', 'Gedoff!') I now added to the list on the board, under the heading 'Words', some new notions: contractions (such as 'can't'), slang (e.g. 'cool'), specialist subject vocabulary, e.g. in lessons, and formality or informality (for example, 'Would you get a pencil?' as opposed to 'Get it, quick'). I explained these terms, which gave able children further detail to use in any future analysis.

I now grouped the children according to their planning skill and recently revealed powers of observation. I asked them, 'How could we investigate this further in school over a week, with fifteen minutes of lesson time per day, plus one final lesson of an hour after that?' I urged them to consider some kind of outcome to show to others (this was problem-solving, as I made clear to the class). In each group, children discussed the possibilities and collaborated in writing them down. They produced notes on one piece of paper per group suggesting at least one method of investigation, on another a method of sharing their research with others.

I collected in the suggestions and stuck them on a display board, anonymised and numbered. (Some groups had had several ideas, thus showing creative thinking; some ideas had gone into significant logistical detail, thus demonstrating skill with problem-solving.) During afternoon 'reassembly time', children took it in turns to scan the board and to put their votes into a ballot box for their preferred investigation and suggested outcome. By the end of the day, having counted the votes, I announced the two favourite suggestions.

Five days of investigation (problem-solving: tackling the challenge)

The winning proposal for an investigation had one group per day visiting another lesson in school as observers. The proposers had even considered in which class observation might be least intrusive, because of its layout and access point from the corridor. Thus (with the agreement of its teacher!) I sent groups with clipboards daily, under adult supervision, to make notes on the conversations they overheard there. Less confident listeners observed the lengths of teacher and pupil utterances, or their volume, or their speed (at my direction). I gave them a code of marks to use to distinguish between long, medium and short, loud, medium and quiet and fast, medium and slow; they jotted these on to paper in separate columns for teacher talk to pupils and pupil talk to teacher. Listeners with more confidence recorded lengths of utterances: not only of teacher to pupils and pupils to teacher but also of pupils to pupils, i.e. making their notes in three columns, not two. When possible, they also noted down the utterances themselves. The most acute listeners recorded examples of slang, informality/formality, subject vocabulary and contractions in the teacher–pupil, pupil–teacher and pupil–pupil columns provided. On their return to their classroom, the children reviewed these notes, trying to code the noted quotations into these three categories – slang, informal/formal and contractions. All found this hard, but a lot of debate was generated.

The winning proposal had suggested another dimension to the investigation: study of talk at playtime. Some keen children continued the exercise then, on fresh pieces of paper, this time dividing their notes into separate columns for supervisory staff talking to children, and children talking to each other (the most observant dividing the latter column into two at my request, for children who were friends or siblings and children who were not).

The final lesson (review: critical thinking, including metacognition)

The class's preferred outcome from this task was to produce a play or plays demonstrating the variety of school talk; however, the Year 4 planning documents did not allow for the time this would take, especially as the class had already studied and written playscripts in an earlier term. Instead, I suggested that groups improvised role-plays, incorporating what they had learnt.

Taking their notes we moved to the hall. There, less confident observers improvised scenes in which a teacher talked to a group of pupils. During these I urged individual actors to demonstrate differences in volume, speed and length of talk, inspired by the lessons they had observed. More confident groups improvised scenes with children talking to each other during a lesson, occasionally interrupted by the teacher: their job was to demonstrate the lengths of utterances and some of the words used. The most confident groups had to show the differences between adult talk with children and children's talk to each other, either in the playground or in a lesson. They had to include examples of slang, formality/informality and contractions.

This was a long lesson, but the children thoroughly enjoyed it and were motivated enough to stay on task throughout. The most able children found their role-plays hard, and despite their observations, often exaggerated teachers' formality of speech! Nonetheless, some interesting insights emerged; for example, they showed that adults, too, speak informally and in broken utterances, e.g. in the playground – the exception being when in 'lecture mode' in teaching/assembly situations! One child had noticed that, even in lessons, children 'chat' informally to each other, and often to the teacher. As the role-plays were performed, I asked the rest of the class as the 'audience' for insights about what we had learnt and how we talked ourselves (metacognition). We recorded these on a poster chart, under the headings 'Length', 'Speed', 'Volume', 'Words'. For example, under 'Length', when asked who uses short utterances and when, one perceptive child noted that two unfamiliar children in the playground might speak shortly to each other, but so might close friends, because they know each other well. Under 'Words' (subdivided into 'Subject vocabulary', 'Slang', 'Informal/formal' and 'Contractions'), one child noted that both a teacher and a lot of children in her lesson might use the 'special words' connected with the subject being studied; another perceptive child, when asked who used contractions and why, could tell me that both teachers and children used them, for speed, all the time.

I then addressed each of my headings, asking whether there was a 'right' length, speed, volume and vocabulary for talk. This generated much debate (critical thinking), leading to the widespread conclusion, as I had hoped, that it depended on the situation. For quite some time after these lessons, children would share with me examples of talk that they had noticed since.

Reading

Many activities in this chapter are equally suited to shared, guided and group reading. A good number of the approaches can also provide a focus where children are reading lengthy texts independently; you may even suggest that they are followed during home reading. Independent reading at home and/or school may also take place over a period of days or weeks *in preparation for* the tasks described.

Where specific texts are mentioned, they are either still in print at the time of writing or 'classic texts', in many school collections. They are given only as examples, and numerous others are equally appropriate.

Problem-solving

The analytical aspect of reading – thinking about the way texts work – is often recognised; it can be seen as critical thinking and problem-solving. But reading involves problem-solving in other ways. Apart from learning to 'decode' print, i.e. to solve the puzzle of the 'grapheme code', children should see that there are deeper puzzles and dilemmas in texts – some with definite 'answers', some without. The following sections suggest ways of encouraging children to explore these.

Finding shapes, finding patterns

Texts have what could be called 'shapes' and 'patterns'. 'Shape' describes the distinctive way in which a text is organised and sequenced, e.g. the text might have an ending that mirrors the beginning in some way, or a discussion text might 'interweave' arguments with counter-arguments. 'Pattern' describes any repetition, e.g. characteristics of the layout that are the same on each page; a consistent rhyme scheme; similar sentence lengths or types of punctuation; a repeated phrase, idea or image; or events that recur in a story. Of course, writers also 'break' patterns for effect. The activities described in the sub-sections below heighten children's awareness of such features. Undertake them when children are familiar with the chosen text/s.

Mapping and tracking
- In much fiction, and some factual recount, people travel through various settings. Ask children to draw pictorial maps showing these journeys. They should draw, by hand or on the computer, each setting visited, with 'pathways' linking them; the travellers can be depicted moving along these routes. From reading

Betsy Byars' short book *The Seven Treasure Hunts*, children can map the young narrator's comical to-ings and fro-ings round his neighbourhood, following and setting treasure-hunt clues; or they can represent the journeyings of Bartlett in Odo Hirsch's novel *Bartlett and the Ice Voyage*. At the challenging end of the spectrum, children can attempt elaborate charts of Lyra and Will's journeyings in Philip Pullman's *His Dark Materials* trilogy. (Maps can be completed over a period of time, as more of the text is read.)

- Alternatively, children can map the 'ballet' of people's meetings, times together and partings (as often recounted in fiction, biography or autobiography). Ask them to illustrate who comes together and when throughout the text, for example beside a timeline, or over background sketches of the settings. Berlie Doherty's *The Snow Queen* should prompt a linear diagram of Kay's encounters, followed by a linear diagram of Gerda's as she sets out to rescue him. Grace Hallworth's short tale 'Kiskadee' relates the various encounters and partings of Flycatcher, Bo Corbeau, Rain-spirit and the other creatures in turn, so lends itself to a chart with radiating 'spokes', each one tracing the meetings of one character with the others. Cornelia Funke's novel *The Thief Lord* also requires a complex chart of relationships, as the story of Victor the detective (and other adults) is partially told in separate chapters from the adventures of the children. Challenge your readers to find their own ways of graphically representing these separate strands.

- Otherwise, ask children to represent the different structures of texts. They might represent these in any combination of appropriate symbols or marks, labelled with key events or elements of the text content. 'Structure diagrams' are especially illuminating if drawn after reading fiction with complex shapes, for instance the two plots of Louis Sachar's *Holes*, which includes an historical background tale; timeslips, e.g. Julia Jarman's short story 'Time Slide' and Charles Ashton's *Time Ghost*, or the flashbacks in Anthony Horowitz's *Scorpia*; stories within the narrative, e.g. Michael Morpurgo's *The Butterfly Lion*, Alison Prince's *The Summerhouse* and Susan Price's *The King's Head*; tales within the narrative that are written or told by characters and which 'tangle with the plot', as in Brian Patten's *The Story Giant*, Geraldine McCaughrean's *A Pack of Lies*, Philip Pullman's *Clockwork*, or *Bambert's Book of Missing Stories* by Reinhardt Jung; and tales told by several tellers, e.g. Michael Lawrence's *The Poppykettle Papers* and Peter Dickinson's epic *The Kin* (which is also interspersed with myths that subtly link to the main narrative). Equally, some non-fiction structures can be represented diagrammatically. Biography, autobiography, journals and diaries can be shown this way, for example revealing how their themes or viewpoints modulate throughout, run in parallel or 'interweave'. Persuasive and discussion texts can be represented diagrammatically as well, for instance showing whether they present arguments grouped together according to theme or point of view; alternating, for example, between 'pros' and 'cons'; 'building up' to a 'climax' of persuasiveness; or beginning with the most forceful reasons, then 'trailing' more minor ones. Sue Palmer's *Skeleton Poster Books*, with their diagrammatic adaptation of a fish-skeleton structure corresponding to each text type, may suggest some ideas; so too may Figure 2.1.

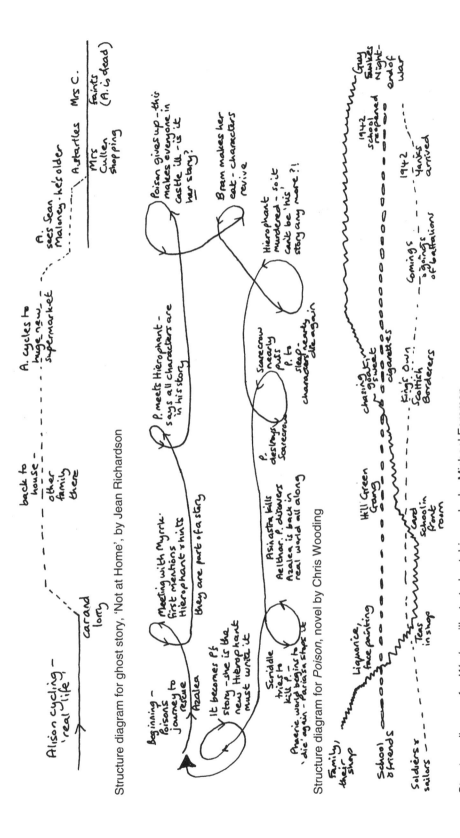

Structure diagram for ghost story, 'Not at Home', by Jean Richardson

Structure diagram for *Poison*, novel by Chris Wooding

Structure diagram for *Warboy*, illustrated autobiography by Michael Foreman

Figure 2.1   Examples of structure diagrams for texts

- At a deeper level, children can 'plot profile' the intended effects of a text on the reader. Get children to chart 'peaks and troughs' in these effects in a line graph (see Figure 2.2), as follows. After the children have read the text, stipulate an effect that you know the writer intends, for example humour, excitement, horror, mystery, sympathy, persuasion or surprise. Ask children to list and number, in chronological sequence, what they consider the most important events from (or sections of) the text. These will correspond to the numbered boxes on the horizontal axis of the graph. The vertical axis represents the chosen 'effect', e.g. surprise. Children should plot with a cross the extent of this effect at all the numbered moments in the text, then join up the crosses. (Children can likewise explore how a writer often achieves several effects, for example persuasion and horror, by using lines in different colours to represent each effect on the same graph.) For example, a story such as Michael Rosen's 'The Bakerloo Flea' has many moments intended to horrify; *The Diary of Anne Frank* engages the reader's sympathy to greater and lesser degrees throughout. Plot profiling can be undertaken bit by bit while reading a text, or as a single task at the end.

Of course, you will need to model and demonstrate these approaches before children try them.

DIFFERENTIATION

Challenge able reader-thinkers to do such tasks independently of any aids (such as those suggested here); give unconfident children a list of the aspects to map, but out of their original sequence: either settings, or characters' meetings and partings, for example, in the case of fiction. If the latter children are attempting a 'structure diagram', show them some ready-drawn diagrams that might 'fit' the text structure, and get them to identify the most appropriate. If attempting plot profiling, give them the numbered list of elements for the horizontal axis.

Comparing and contrasting

Supply children with a grid to help them to compare and contrast features within one text, or across several. You can invite them, in pairs or groups, simply to compare and contrast orally, using the headings in the grid as prompts. Alternatively, you can ask them to fill in each box with their ideas. (See Figures 2.3–2.5.)

In stories, children can compare and contrast settings, plotlines or characters' personalities. The ways in which different authors describe the landscape in two pieces of fiction set in the same historical period can be placed side by side; so can two fantasy settings, for example Philip Reeve's in *Mortal Engines* with Rhiannon Lassiter's in *Hex*; or adapt Figure 2.3 to allow children to compare the fantasy world of a text with the real world, e.g. the landscape of *The Wind Singer* trilogy by William Nicholson, or that of Malorie Blackman in *Noughts and Crosses*. Challenge children to compare and distinguish between the 'shape of events' in a variety of Greek or Roman myths. The severe-seeming yet perceptive and sympathetic Miss Minton, in Eva Ibbotson's *Journey to the River Sea*, can be viewed alongside Polly Horvath's portrait of the boring and severe school counsellor Miss Honeycut, in

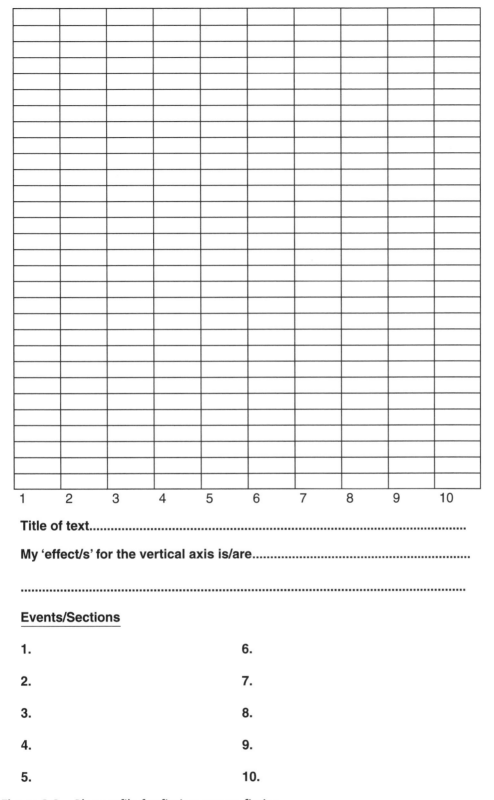

| | 1 | 2 | 3 | 4 | 5 | 6 | 7 | 8 | 9 | 10 |

Title of text...

My 'effect/s' for the vertical axis is/are...

....

Events/Sections

1.   6.

2.   7.

3.   8.

4.   9.

5.   10.

Figure 2.2 Plot profile for fiction or non-fiction

Everything on a Waffle; or Aunts Sponge and Spiker compared in Roald Dahl's *James and the Giant Peach*. While reading a text describing a world faith, or various social groups in an historical period or another part of the world, ask children to use a version of Figure 2.4 to compare people's lifestyles and viewpoints. Use a

Title of story text or texts.............................

	Characters [fill in details] • First and outward impressions (voice, looks, etc.) • Personality	Settings [fill in details] • How they are described • How important they are in the story	Things that happen [fill in details] • Which and how many characters have 'main stories' • What kinds of events and setbacks • The 'shape' of the main events • What themes	Techniques the author uses • What kinds of description, imagery • What kinds of speech • What narrative viewpoint/s (whose thoughts and feelings the reader knows)
What is the same about them?				
What is different about them?				

Figure 2.3   Grid for comparing and contrasting aspects of stories. You can enlarge this, or choose one or two columns only

Title of non-fiction text or texts....................

Several groups of people (or several people) [fill in details]	Their background, homes, home settings etc.	The way they live/d	Their beliefs or opinions	Beliefs or opinions of the author (and how you know)
What is/was the same about them?				
What is/was different about them?				

Figure 2.4   Grid for comparing and contrasting people through non-fiction. You can enlarge this, choose one or two columns only and edit headings to fit the task

Titles of poems..

	What they are about • People, things, places, situations, feelings • Themes and ideas	What form they are written in, e.g. haiku, limerick, blank verse • Pattern of stanzas, rhythms and rhyme • Layout on page	What kinds of language and punctuation, e.g. speech, simile, metaphor, description, informal, questions, exclamations, what tense, no commas	Effect/s on the reader, e.g. surprise, humour, thought-provoking
What is the same about them?				
What is different about them?				

Figure 2.5   Grid for comparing and contrasting poems. You can enlarge this, or choose one or two columns only

different grid, with two columns headed 'Facts' and 'Opinions' and no 'Same/different' division, to encourage readers to distinguish the bias in a purportedly informative text. Tony Mitton's 'Secret Passage' and 'Forbidden Poem', in his poetry collection *Plum*, with their different tones but common theme (literature as an entry point to a different world), can likewise stimulate interesting comparisons (using a grid such as in Figure 2.5).

Finally, Figure 2.3 can be adjusted to enable children to compare versions of a text in different formats or media, for example the cartoon-strip version by Marcia Williams of a Shakespeare play with a prose or play version; one of J. K. Rowling's *Harry Potter* novels with the corresponding film; or Morris Gleitzman's *Two Weeks with the Queen* with the six-part play adaptation.

DIFFERENTIATION

Encourage able reader-thinkers to work independently, and/or to use a fairly detailed grid format. Put unsure children with trusted peers. If they are recording thoughts on a grid, ensure unconfident writers are with more confident children who can scribe for them.

Categorising and classifying

The sub-sections below suggest two 'textual levels' at which to use this activity.

Sentences and paragraphs

While reading a text, ask children to find a way of classifying sentences or paragraphs within it. They should place them in two or more groups by recording them in separate columns, labelling them with annotated Post-it® notes or underlining them with different-coloured pens. Suggest that they separate out:

- sentences according to the different effects they have on the reader;
- sentences with different levels of complexity (e.g. very short and very long, or simple, compound and complex);
- sentences according to the order of word classes within them (nouns, verbs, adjectives, adverbs, prepositions);
- sentences according to the types and/or variety of punctuation within them;
- dialogue according to the purpose it serves (e.g. moving the story forward, giving information about relationships, revealing characters' moods and feelings);
- direct and reported speech according to the purposes they serve (e.g. moving the story forward, speeding up events, avoiding repetition, giving information about relationships, revealing characters' moods and feelings);
- sections of a non-fiction text according to their purpose (e.g. information, general introduction, explanation, persuasion); or
- paragraphs according to how they 'move the text on' (e.g. progressing to new ideas or reasons, a new time, place or person, or into speech).

Ask children what this exercise shows them. Does the writer employ a variety of sentences/paragraphs (according to the children's sorting method), or a limited range? What reasons do writers seem to have for using such variety?

Whole texts

Present children, preferably in groups or pairs, with several texts. These might be extracts, short and complete texts or whole books. Select texts that will encourage readers to classify them either:

- According to where they would fit in your school library classification system, e.g. Dewey. Their decisions should be based solely on scanning the book (e.g. any cover, blurb, contents page, illustrations, layout or headings), and skimming the body text, not on a 'close read'. Or

- According to genre. This can involve distinguishing, say, myths from traditional and modern tales, or explanation texts from information (reports). It could, however, be more challenging, for instance classifying texts as either myths, legends or fables; deciding on several sub-categories for fantasy; or teasing out the relationship between mysteries, ghost stories, horror stories, thrillers and detective stories. Or

- According to the effect on the reader. The children could classify newspaper or magazine articles according to their point of view on a common subject; distinguish between different types of comedy (slapstick, word-play, etc.); or examine the functions in fiction of different stock characters (hero, anti-hero, sidekick, mysterious stranger, etc.).

DIFFERENTIATION

Within any of these activities, more able children may benefit from a more open-ended challenge. Suggest that they decide on their *own* reasons for grouping the texts (though you might select the sentences/paragraphs/texts for them to examine). Unconfident children should work in pairs or groups.

In how few . . .?

. . . words?

Use this activity when children have finished reading a story, poem or play that presents one or more themes, issues or moral messages. Ask these readers, perhaps with a partner, to find the fewest possible words to sum up the 'point' of the text *without telling any story, or describing the text*. Ask children listening to their ideas to stop them if they 'begin to explain' what they have read. For instance, the theme of Shaun Tan's sophisticated picture book *The Red Tree* might be summed up as 'hope triumphing over despair'. The issue (a 'theme that is a problem') in Libby Hathorn's thought-provoking picture book *Way Home* is young people's homelessness; in Elizabeth Laird's *Secret Friends*, the issues are racial prejudice and bullying. The unstated message of Hilaire Belloc's poem about Matilda is

'Don't tell lies', and of Aesop's fable 'The Tortoise and the Hare', 'Going slowly but surely often pays off.'

You can challenge individuals or pairs to compete to find the fewest possible words for their summing-up.

DIFFERENTIATION

Leave this task open for able thinkers; give uncertain thinkers a selection of possible themes or 'messages', some appropriate, some not, e.g. on folded pieces of paper. Invite them to pick the most suitable, and give their reasons why.

. . . steps?

Use this 'adversarial' activity when children are reading non-fiction texts. It is especially suitable for the start of cross-curricular research, e.g. about ancient Egypt, places of worship or famous inventions. Children should work in pairs. Ask child A in each pair to find an interesting fact in a book consulted, without revealing to their partner B where in the book they found it. A then relates the fact, challenging B to locate it in as few steps as possible, for example by going from the index to the right page, to the appropriate headed section, to the right line of text. Indexes are not always comprehensive, or can give multiple page references, and page layouts are often complex or misleading, which is what makes this activity challenging: warn children that they may encounter such difficulties. Each 'searcher' *must* relate out loud the steps they are taking. Partners then exchange roles and repeat the game. (If you like, use timers too, thus introducing a 'race' element!) A variant of this is to ask children to work in competing pairs on the Internet, finding facts in as few steps as they can on particular websites. If desired, you can ask searchers to record their 'steps' in note form or in a flow-chart diagram.

On visits to the school library, supply children with 'treasure hunt' cards: questions to research by racing to find a suitable text and then the page on which the answer can be found.

DIFFERENTIATION

This activity is harder or easier depending on the books or websites used: the more dense and sophisticated the text, the less comprehensive or systematic its cross-referencing and the more complex its layout, the more challenging the activity becomes. More adventurous readers can set the fact-finding for their partners as questions, e.g. 'In what year was . . .?'

Solving puzzles, using clues

In texts at Key Stage 2, children need textual 'puzzles' about which they can theorise. Set children the task of 'solving' these puzzles when they read. Always encourage readers to support their ideas with evidence (details in pictures, quotations, etc.). The sub-sections below suggest several approaches.

What's the connection?

This activity especially suits kinaesthetic learners, and promotes active learning. When children are about to read a text, provide them with an artefact obliquely associated with it. For example:

- to accompany an explanation text about what smoking does to the lungs, a fragment of tarmac;

- beside a report text about the ozone layer, a piece of translucent holey fabric;

- along with a persuasive text about the benefits of exercise, a TV guide;

- when studying a timeline, fossils and fragments of pottery from different periods;

- if reading Anne Frank's Diary, a heart locket locked in a box (to represent her life in hiding and love for Peter);

- to illuminate Roger McGough's poem 'First Day at School', a little yellow Wellington boot (which has symbolic meaning in the poem); or

- to highlight the bond between Ramona and her mother in Beverly Cleary's novel of the same name, a bottle of floral scent (alongside the episode where daughter tries to leave home, and mother, with her heartstring-tugging flower fragrance, thwarts her).

During reading, ask children to consider in how many ways the artefact is connected with the text (e.g. the TV guide may contain programmes about exercise, as well as representing the 'couch potato' syndrome). After reading, invite children to share these ideas; they must justify them. Praise wide-ranging and thoughtful responses.

DIFFERENTIATION

The more obliquely connected the artefact, the more challenging the task. Thus it is more straightforward to make the link between a pot of honey and an explanation text about insect pollination than it is to associate a jacket with dog hairs on it with the same text (even though it could symbolise the process of 'accidental transportation' of pollen).

What does it mean?

Get children to read texts in which the ending, or some element of the content, has to be inferred. (Some texts are ambiguous, suggesting various interpretations.) For instance:

- Readers of the ending to Melvyn Burgess's sophisticated picture book *The Birdman* will need to work out for themselves that the boy Jarvis, now a bird, is being cruelly punished for having kept a robin imprisoned.

- Judy Allen's picture book *Tiger* turns out to narrate not the attempts of a hunter to kill the creature but a photographer's admiring 'shots' of it and his desire for its survival. Children must infer this.

- In Jamie Rix's short story 'The New Nanny', two troublesome children get their nanny fired. They subject succeeding nannies – a python and a spider – to untold torments, and are then persecuted by an alligator nanny in turn. They eventually welcome their original nanny back – with her suitcases of snake, spider and alligator skin. What, children can consider, does this ending mean?

- David Almond's novel *Skellig* should provoke readers to wonder, just what is Skellig?

- A few chapters into Sally Prue's *Cold Tom*, ask children to explain what the 'Tribe' and the 'demons' are, justifying their answers.

- Prompted by Charles Causley's poem 'Why?', children can debate the reasons for Susanna's horror at seeing the guy on the bonfire. Invite them to invent possible traumas she has suffered.

- Ask children who 'The Listeners' might be in Walter de la Mare's poem. What might be their story? What might be the Traveller's 'word' he says he 'kept', and why has he come? What might he and the Listeners look like?

- Look at Ted Hughes's unpunctuated, puzzling poem 'Grizzly Bear'. Ask children first to pool the mental images they get. Then ask them what is happening throughout. Challenge them to brainstorm as many ideas as possible. Is the poem even about a bear?

- Get the children to examine any story or poem that includes a strong dialect, or a nonsense poem. Ask them to attempt, orally, their own 'translation', and to justify it to others using details from the text.

- Conceal the title of a poem or short story that the children are reading. Ask them to suggest their own, justifying them with reference to the text. (When the title is revealed, they may well feel that some of their own ideas are better!)

DIFFERENTIATION

For the deepest thinkers, choose texts where there is scope for ambiguity, different interpretations or debate. Ask the most astute to identify the 'puzzles' for themselves, without pre-setting them questions about the texts. If you do question able thinkers, leave your questioning open. Provide the least confident thinkers with several ideas or interpretations of your own, some of which do not 'fit' the text. Ask them to choose one. They must justify this with close reference to the text.

Exploring dilemmas

Stories, plays, recounts and narrative or dialogue poems often describe characters or real-life people in difficult situations. In particular, moral dilemmas are useful to explore. For example, in Susan Gates's novelette *Waiting for Goldie*, Danny has to decide whether or how to tell Grandad, dangerously ill in hospital, that his champion racing pigeon is missing. A transcript of the *Titanic* disaster hearings reveals the quandary of Mr Pitman, an officer in charge of a lifeboat, about whether to approach the ship again to pick up more passengers. In Valerie Bloom's poem 'Sandwich', a child going on a school trip wrestles with the social embarrassment of a grandmother intent on equipping her with a hearty meal instead of the sandwich the teacher has requested.

Ask children to stop reading any such text at the point where the problem has been presented, and then:

- brainstorm ideas for solutions, in pairs or as a group. They can then suggest their favourite option. Or

- explore the dilemma through hotseating. An adult or peer can play the part of the person in difficulties. In role they can question the group, and be questioned and advised in turn. Or

- make a 'conscience alley'. A peer or adult can represent the troubled individual. Other children, in two lines forming an arch, should suggest ideas, pros and cons as the 'character' passes through. Or

- role-play the situation as the various characters, exploring what might best resolve things.

Stress that you are not asking the children to 'second-guess' the outcome of the original text, but to be independent-thinking, practical and, possibly, imaginative. They should consider the moral issues from all sides. Their suggested solutions must 'fit' the details of the text. Afterwards, the rest of the text should be read. Ask readers to discuss whose solutions to the dilemma they favour.

DIFFERENTIATION

Ensure your questioning of able children is open to a variety of solutions; support unconfident children by suggesting a few solutions yourself, some practical or 'moral', some the reverse, and some that do not fit the details of the scenario. Encourage them to select from your examples.

Creative thinking

When is a—not a—?

Ask children to find varied examples of one element from their reading, for instance of a:

- sentence;

- question;

- character type frequently found in fiction, e.g. a witch, unpleasant teacher, detective, ghost;

- dialogue;

- poetic form, e.g. haiku, limerick;
- explanation; or
- glossary.

Ask them to consider the 'rules' that make that element what it is, for example, by brainstorming with a partner, colour-highlighting or writing a list of key features. Then invite them to find or devise an example that breaks some of these 'rules'. Encourage them to be daring and imaginative, probing with questions such as 'How different can *x* be?', 'When is an *x* not an *x*?' For instance, in the case of sentences that 'break rules', children might suggest one-word 'sentences', 'sentences' in note form, or 'sentences' without verbs; in the case of witches, a witch who has some very unwitch-like qualities; as an instance of unusual dialogue, texting, with its abbreviated spellings and missing speech marks; in the case of haiku, a haiku laid out in a single line; or in the case of glossaries, a glossary with several levels of difficulty, to cater for different readers. Children should express their ideas verbally, or – if they are recorded – in note form only: this is an activity to stimulate creative readers, not creative writers.

DIFFERENTIATION

Ask able children to find varied examples of texts that break the rules; if children need more support, or time is short, provide texts that contain 'rule-breaking' instances yourself. Do not ask children to invent their own unusual and unexpected cases unless they are especially confident and imaginative. If they are doing this, some children may need illustrative instances, for example if they are considering ideas for untypical questions, you can model the activity by giving examples of untypical exclamations; if they are considering ideas for unstereotypical ghosts, you can explain how witches might break their stereotypes.

Elaborate on . . .

. . . *the story*

Use this activity with fiction, narrative poetry or plays. Identify a character in a text who 'leaves the action' halfway-through, a setting 'deserted' by the characters at some juncture, or an artefact mentioned only briefly by the author. When this point is reached in the text, or later, after a complete reading, ask children to make up a story for that character, setting or artefact. (This might or might not include some elements of the original narrative.) Children might explore their ideas through role-play, drawing, storytelling or discussion. Do not oblige them to write the story, but ask them to think of an intriguing title. They should 'flesh their ideas out', orally or pictorially, with as much detail as possible. They can discuss whether, if ever written down, their stories would have the same mood, style, form or genre as the text that inspired them. As an extension, share the resultant list of titles with the class, or another audience who knows the original text (e.g. on a poster). This audience can vote on the stories they most wish had been written.

. . . the arguments

Apply this activity to any persuasive or discussion text that the children have just read. In the case of persuasive text, ask children to brainstorm and/or record in list form any other arguments or reasons that the writer could have used. A wider audience, e.g. another group or the teacher, can be invited to judge which of these omitted arguments is the most compelling. In the case of discussion text, ask children to think of as many other points of view on the subject as possible. They should then brainstorm and/or record in a table the sets of arguments they associate with each point of view. (An initial role-played debate or discussion may help.) Again, a wider audience, such as another group or the teacher, can be invited to judge which of the omitted viewpoints comes across as most significant, based on the strength and number of arguments the children have attributed to it.

DIFFERENTIATION

For the activities above, give able thinkers a fairly open brief, but less certain thinkers tighter parameters for the task, e.g.:

- With the activity based on narrative, stipulate some ingredients that must come into their new story outline, e.g. suggest some details about one or two characters or settings or events not in the original story.

- With the activity based on argument, stipulate the new point of view to be explored; encourage children simply to brainstorm the arguments that could be used by someone with this viewpoint.

Creative urges

While or after studying a text, ask children to think of one thing that this reading experience *makes them want to do*. Give them highly varied examples of possible answers, illustrating the potential scope of response, e.g. become a footballer; read shorter texts, or different kinds of text; find out more about the subject or the author; look at fairgrounds in a new way; read it in a different way next time (e.g. silently, or omitting some parts); use some element from the text in their own writing, e.g. a word, a character or a setting; see a film version of the text, or make one; or look up a word.

Ask them what it was *precisely* about the text or reading experience that made them feel this. (This part of their answer is vital. As long as negative responses are explained in detail, they can be welcomed.) If children keep any kind of reading journal, they may answer this question periodically in writing – indeed several times, at different points, if reading longer texts. As a variant on this activity, ask children to speculate about someone they know well: what do the children think the text would make this other person want to do, and why?

As a further variant, ask children to select one thing about the text that they would change (e.g. a phrase, the ending, the tense, the absence of rhyme, the organisation of the text), and to give their reasons. They should also state *how* they would change that aspect. Again, such ideas can be recorded in reading journals. When this exploration takes place as a group discussion, urge children not to echo each other's ideas, but encourage each to strive to select something different.

DIFFERENTIATION

The open questioning above is most suited to able thinkers; to be more supportive, concentrate on one of the ideas listed on page 54 and ask children questions around it, e.g.:

- what ambitions, if any, the text gives them;

- what other kinds of texts they would like to read, having read this one;

- one thing they would like to find out more about, having read the text;

- how they would like to read the text next time, if they were asked to;

- what element of the text they might use in their own writing (a word, phrase, character, event, etc.);

- how the text could be made into a film, and what changes might have to be made; or

- which words or phrases they would like to investigate further.

Ensure you ask them *what in the text* makes them respond as they do.

Making black white (or at least much whiter)

Once children have studied a text, ask them to consider in detail what alterations would be needed *throughout* a text to achieve an opposite, or very different, effect, for example:

- turning a happy ending into a sad one, or vice-versa;

- converting a balanced discussion into a persuasive argument;

- giving a poem a different form;

- changing the mood of a piece of scene-setting;

- adapting a dictionary for younger/older readers;

- giving a fictional character a different personality;

- changing instructions into advice; or

- making a formal text informal.

Children should brainstorm their ideas, i.e. work orally; if you would like a record of their thoughts, ask them to do a rough list of the changes they consider necessary, or roughly to edit a photocopy of the text (this is a reading-based, not a writing, activity). Pair or group work, for most children, will be more stimulating and productive than working individually.

What could be the question with this answer?

These activities can be useful for summative or formative assessment.

Give children just one of these 'answers':

- adjectives (or verbs, adverbs or proper nouns);
- synonyms (or antonyms or homonyms);
- similes (or metaphors);
- a colon (or a semi-colon);
- complex sentences; or;
- the author/poet/illustrator/publisher (fill in the blank with a name with a substantial oeuvre, e.g. Jacqueline Wilson, Kevin Crossley-Holland, Gareth Owen, Chris Van Allsburg, the publisher Dorling Kindersley).

Set them the task of deciding what the 'question' could have been that prompted such an answer. Stress that there is *no right question*. The best ones will be unlike other children's, and quite detailed. Children need to design their questions through close scrutiny of one or more appropriate texts (e.g. if the 'answer' is similes, their texts should contain a variety of types of simile). Children should already understand any concept contained in the 'answer', e.g. complex sentence, adjective. They can work individually or in pairs, orally or in writing – whichever you feel will produce best results.

You can also limit the challenge by providing only one appropriate passage or text from which to research the question.

Finally, some children will benefit from 'oral frames' when wording questions. Verbalise them, or display them in the classroom, as appropriate. Some might be:

- What do (children must give their list) have in common?
- What is the same about (children must give their list)?
- In (name of text), what can you say about (children must give examples)?

Design a project on . . .

Give children a 'literacy theme' to research through reading. Examples include:

- formal and informal language;
- the layout of dialogue;
- the reasons why authors use dialogue;
- a particular word root or word roots;
- silent letters in spelling;
- a specific punctuation mark;
- technical or specialist vocabulary – on a topic of the children's choice, or yours;
- reading between the lines: what goes unsaid in texts;
- a particular story genre, e.g. fables, myths from different cultures; or
- thesauruses.

Ask children – in groups, in pairs or individually – to plan:

1 What they want to know about the theme.
2 What texts, websites and other resources they may use for their research.
3 How they will do research, sharing out any tasks.
4 How they will document or present their findings.
5 How they will timetable the enterprise, in consultation with you.

It is often useful to continue the project at home.

Of course, designing a project also entails problem-solving; however, devising the format in which to showcase the results requires creative thinking in particular. Some options children might choose are:

- an interview or role-played TV programme;
- a captioned display;
- photographs or pictures;
- an information leaflet;
- a talk or group presentation, with 'props' or illustrations; or
- a scrapbook of captioned examples.

> ## DIFFERENTIATION
>
> Children unsure about organisation – who may include some of the more able – will need you to set the timetable (and perhaps to monitor their progress). For others, self-organisation may provide the ideal challenge. You may wish to specify particular questions to research, e.g. for a word root: 'Which language does it come from?', 'What did it mean originally?', 'How many words can you find that use it?', 'How are they all connected with the original meaning?', 'How does this knowledge help with spelling them?', 'Can you invent some new words with this root?' To help further, you may stipulate or provide the books and websites to be used to research the theme. Finally, for less confident workers, you limit the choice of formats listed on page 57 in which they may present their findings (do not however *dictate* one: this would curtail the 'creative thinking' element).

After the children's presentations, you may wish to study a chosen theme further with the class.

Bring together . . .

Children can work individually, in pairs or groups for any of the three sub-categories of this activity, detailed below.

. . . *features of fiction*

Pick a feature that children can search for and compare across different texts, for example: heroes/heroines; characters who are outcasts; school settings; mysteries and puzzles; twists in stories; cliffhanger endings; distinctive ways of speaking; historical language. Brief them to collect as many examples as they can from different sources, e.g. by bookmarking them in books or online or circling them on photocopied pages. Ask them what they have learnt about the range that authors use. An extension of this is to invite children to invent a 'hybrid' of the feature studied, e.g. a new kind of hero, or a cliffhanger with a twist.

. . . *aspects of poetry*

Pick an aspect that children can search for and compare across a variety of poems, for example: rhyme schemes; narratives in poetry; lists. Brief them to collect as many examples as they can from different sources. Ask them what they have learnt from finding such a variety of poems with this feature. An extension of this is to invite children to invent something new from what they have discovered: *not* to write a new poem (a writing activity) but, for example, to map out a plan for a new rhyme scheme, or to think of an unusual theme for a narrative or list poem.

. . . *information from non-fiction*

Pick a research topic (possibly one being studied anyway), for example 'Forces'. Ask children to select a sub-theme, e.g. pushes, pulls, forces in sport, natural forces, forces in building. Brief them to find information on this theme from as many sources as they can: books and/or websites, pictures *and* text – the more disparate the sources, the more challenging the task. They can bookmark useful pages or websites, or circle relevant information, if downloaded or on photocopies. Then ask them to collate the information into some new (largely non-written) form, e.g. a demonstration, an oral presentation, a model, or informative drawings with captions. Children must be able to show that they have 'fused' their findings into this new product.

> ## DIFFERENTIATION
>
> In all three activities above, allow able researchers to research from a wide variety of texts and sources. If children have limited research skills, pre-select the texts they should consult, and their length. However, all pupils will need several texts (at least two), so group the less confident with more capable researchers if necessary. The challenge comes in asking them to generalise from, or collate together, the particular information found.

Critical thinking

Many of the activities described below can follow on from many of those described in the 'Problem-solving' and 'Creative thinking' sections of this chapter. Most can equally stand alone.

Rating and choosing

While reading, or using certain texts for reference, ask children to identify and rate (for example as first, second and third):

- in a dictionary, the 'top' letters of the alphabet – for example, on the basis of their frequency as the initial letter in words (or the 'top' combinations of two or three initial letters);
- the 'top' words, phrases, lines or sentences in any newly read prose or poem – for instance, on the basis of which seem to represent the text best, or which are readers' favourites, or least favourite;
- the 'top' texts out of several (websites, magazines, non-fiction, poems, novels in a series or texts by one author) – for example, on the basis of which are most useful for reference on a subject, or which are the clearest, the most persuasive, objective, exciting or funny;
- the 'top' parts of a text – for instance, on the basis of which arguments are most persuasive, or which passages in fiction are most atmospheric or frightening; or
- the 'top' genres of fiction – perhaps based on readers' preferences.

The children should justify their rankings. In further variants of this task:

- Ask children to rate their invented titles for a text whose original title you have concealed (an activity suggested in the 'Creative thinking' section): which is their preferred title, second favourite and so on?
- Invite individuals to rate and discuss their own 'reading performance' during several recent occasions of guided or group reading.

Instead of ranking, children can simply identify their number one choice. You might express this task as a question: 'If you could "buy" only one *x*, which would it be?' Urge them to justify its selection.

In another variant, ask children to use a 'Comparing and contrasting' grid, similar to those in Figures 2.3–2.5 in the 'Problem-solving' section on pages 44–46, to show their preference of one text over another. In place of 'What is the same about them?' and 'What is different about them?', substitute the headings, 'What do you prefer from one text?' and 'What makes it better, for you, than the other?'

DIFFERENTIATION

Invite adventurous thinkers and readers to do one of the above rating activities using a criterion of their own, e.g. favourite, least favourite, funniest, clearest, most frightening, most boring, most persuasive, most complex, longest, shortest, most heavily punctuated, most frequent, most surprising, most unusual, most difficult to understand. They can also write up their ratings in reading journals (see below, under 'Evaluations', page 63).

Recommendations

At least initially, ask children to practise reading recommendations orally, e.g. by addressing a partner or a group (written reviews are primarily a writing, not a reading challenge). Where possible they should make them to a motivating audience, e.g. a friend who does not know about the recommended 'item', a reading buddy in an older/younger class or sceptical peers! Some ideas for recommendations are:

- the 'top three' – or one – chosen item/s from a 'rating and choosing' activity described on page 59;

- a favourite subject in non-fiction (e.g. engines, riding);

- a preferred method of selecting reading books; or

- tips for reading or using a particular text or type of text, e.g. a favourite poem, a DIY manual, a gaming magazine, a catalogue, a travel brochure, a website, a chatroom or an information book.

Ensure that readers explain *why* they are making their recommendations.

DIFFERENTIATION

Allow confident speakers freedom as to how to structure their talks. Get confident reader-writers occasionally to write their recommendations into any reading journal they keep (see below, under 'Evaluations', page 63). These could begin with a summary or description of the 'item', before moving on to list 'what is good' about it. At other times, ask readers who need an extra challenge to play devil's advocate, i.e. to find 'good things' to recommend even in a genre, text or passage they did *not* enjoy.

Suggest to children who need support such speaking frames as 'You would really like/enjoy . . . because', 'The special thing about *x* is . . .' or 'The reason I chose *x* is . . .'. Rephrase your questioning about *why* readers are making certain recommendations if they find 'Why?' questions hard. Ask instead, '*What* do you like/find exciting, helpful, etc. about *x*?' (This directs readers to list or quote specific aspects of their reading.) If they are recommending a text, or part of one, it may help if they describe three important parts of, or events in, that text first.

Polarities

After reading a text or a self-contained part of one (e.g. a chapter), give the children a shuffled pack of cards, each bearing one word from the following pairs of opposing value-judgement words:

- right/wrong;
- good/bad;
- agree/disagree;
- like/dislike;
- easy/difficult;
- strong/weak;
- persuasive/unconvincing;
- true/false;
- objective/biased; and
- pro/con.

You may need to ensure that certain meanings are understood, e.g. 'objective'. You may also wish to exclude some word cards, depending on the text read; for example, the last four pairs listed above are particularly suited to readings of non-fiction texts that express or imply points of view.

Invite the children to pick a card at random; challenge them to make statements – either about some aspect of the text read, e.g. a character described, an effect created by the author or an argument outlined, or of their own reading performance – using the word they have chosen. (Some will prove hard to use, and require ingenuity!) They must justify their statements with reasons or details; they can also build on each other's ideas, for instance, 'It is *false* that all birds nest in trees because I have heard of some that nest at ground-level', or 'I *disagree* with James that the author creates a calm atmosphere: I think it is spooky because of phrases like "the dead eyes of the house".'

This activity is particularly suited to guided or group reading of a shared text. Ask each reader around the group to take turns to pick a card and have their say.

Evaluations

The following sub-sections describe two different approaches to evaluation.

Judging

After you or the children have read a text or a self-contained part of one (e.g. a chapter), canvass their judgements on one or two of the following. Ask them whether:

- they would keep it in or out of a small imaginary 'reading suitcase';
- they liked or disliked it (and how much, e.g. on a scale of 1 to 5);
- they found it boring or entertaining/interesting (and how much, e.g. on a scale);
- they thought it was funny (and how funny, e.g. on a scale);
- it held any surprises;
- it made them want to hear/read more (of the text, in the same genre or vein or by the same author);
- they found it hard to follow/read (and if so, how hard); and/or
- they liked or disliked your/their own 'reading performance' (and how much).

Ask children for a show of hands for or against, or undertake a 'secret ballot' on pieces of paper. Welcome diverse responses: celebrate non-conformity. Over a period of time, you may wish to build up a star rating system for texts read in a group or class.

Reading journals

Ask reader-writers to keep journals in which to record their judgements and opinions of their reading (perhaps using existing home-school diaries, or thinking/learning logs). In order to promote thoughtful, critical entries, insert in these books in advance a list of generic questions, for example for fiction:

- Describe a character: what is special about them, or why is he/she a favourite of yours?

- Describe a setting: what does the author make you feel about it, and how?

- Choose an event that you found exciting, funny or surprising: why?

- Which three sentences or phrases did you notice especially? What did you think about them? What effect do you think the author was trying to create?

- List any words you did not know or found hard. How did you work them out?

- After your reading, write down what you think might happen next. Next time, record how close your prediction was. What, if anything, surprised you?

- What kind of book/text is this? Does it remind you of any others, films, TV programmes, etc. ('intertextuality')? What do you like or dislike about it so far?

And for non-fiction:

- How much did you know about this subject before reading? What would you like to find out? By the end of this read, did you?

- What do you think of the design and layout?

- Has your read taught you any new words or phrases? What do they mean?

- Which parts of the text, if any, did you find hard? How did you work them out?

- Try looking things up in this text. What did you search for? How easy is it to find your way around?

Ask children when reading independently, e.g. at home, to choose one of these items and to respond to it in writing. Alternatively, select an item for them. (Next time, they should write about a different item.) You might like to add the questions about themselves as readers listed on pp. 70–71, plus one final question:

- How easy do you find it to write about your reading? What do you find hard?

These focus on metacognition.

The rating and choosing activities, and the idea of recommendations, all described on pages 59 and 60, can equally stimulate particular types of entry in a reading journal.

DIFFERENTIATION

Encourage able reader-writers to respond in their own way to the questions set, or to adapt your writing frames; these can be given to the less confident if necessary, e.g. 'I tried looking up *x* in this book by . . . This worked/didn't work because . . .'. For children unfamiliar with keeping reading journals you will need to model writing your own entry or entries first, expressing personal observations on a text or texts you have read yourself.

What to do differently?

After reading a text to or with children, ask them:

- what the author could do to make a particular character (or events) funnier, more interesting, less frightening or less predictable;
- how the writer could make his/her language more unusual, interesting, descriptive or beautiful to listen to;
- in what ways the layout of a text, the pictures, a book cover or blurb could be made more attractive or easier to follow; or
- how the reader/s could improve their 'reading performance', whether aloud or silent, for next time.

DIFFERENTIATION

Invite able critical thinkers to incorporate these ideas into a letter or e-mail to the author or publisher of the text. On the other hand, if you have asked them to consider improvements for their own future 'reading performances', ask them to jot down their thoughts in their reading journals. They should re-read these notes before the next similar reading begins; encourage them to try to improve in the light of their self-evaluations. Invite other children to label copies of the text with their suggestions in brief note form or using a code, for example for a classroom display.

How was it?

Before they begin to read any text not previously seen, prime children to be alert to:

- how they feel when they first see the text and know they are going to read it;
- in the case of a story, what they think when they encounter the opening of the text, and the first character, setting or event;
- in fiction, how they think differently as they encounter further characters, settings or events;
- in the case of non-fiction, what they think or do when they encounter facts and features (e.g. 'did you know?' panels or fonts) they didn't expect;
- whether some aspects of the text remind them of other texts, films, TV programmes, personal experiences, etc., and how ('intertextuality');
- how they react if faced with vocabulary they don't know, textual links or sentence constructions they find hard; and/or
- whether they feel differently, or are surprised, as they read more.

After the read, ask them to relate to you or others these feelings and impressions (metacognition). Alternatively, ask them to 'map' this changing process in some way, for example, as annotations in the margins of the text, or as notes or a flow diagram on a separate sheet of paper, to share afterwards with others. Praise readers' honesty, and especially their readiness to describe different thought processes from their peers.

DIFFERENTIATION

If reading independently, confident reader-writers can note their various reactions in a reading journal (see page 63). Later, if they belong to a group that is reading a common text, they might read and discuss their entries in that group. Alternatively, they can devise a code of 'reaction symbols' and flag the text with Post-it® notes bearing these at appropriate points.

Ask less confident readers to feed back on only one or two of the points above. Alternatively, ask them to sticker with Post-it® notes the points in the text where they encounter the first character, setting or event, subsequent new features, unknown facts, unexpected elements, surprises, reminders of other texts or experiences, or difficult vocabulary (label these in advance with appropriate headings, e.g. 'First character', 'Reminder of another text'). They can record on each sticker (or tell you later) how they reacted at these points, e.g. 'I looked up the word in the glossary at the back', 'I carried on reading in the hope I would understand later' or 'I re-read the previous pages to try to make sense of it.'

Affective thinking and emotional literacy

Tracking thoughts and feelings . . .

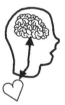

At Key Stage 1, in a range of learning contexts, your fellow teachers may have drawn children's attention to the wide variety of human emotions – anger, fear, happiness, anxiety, surprise, like, dislike, and so on. Teachers and children may have considered together the differences in people's body language and behaviour when experiencing each feeling, and the kinds of situations that provoke them. Ideally, by Key Stage 2 children should be aware that no emotions are 'bad' – that all are valid in certain contexts, but may need to be managed and controlled.

You may, however, need to initiate or consolidate such work yourself. If so, begin by introducing a basic list of some of the most common emotions (e.g. those mentioned above). Work with children to devise corresponding emoticons (facial expression symbols intended to convey different feelings). These can be displayed, for instance on a classroom poster, and used not only in literacy but in many cross-curricular contexts. In literacy itself, when reading fiction children can stick Post-it® notes bearing emoticons next to dialogue that they feel betrays specific emotions in the characters; when thinking critically about texts, they can draw like/dislike emoticons beside phrases or sentences that evoke these feelings in them as readers, and 'puzzlement' emoticons beside text they do not understand.

Before undertaking some of the approaches outlined in the sub-sections below, Key Stage 2 children will need to be familiar with a wider, subtler range of emotions: introduce and discuss the meanings of such feelings as bravado, shyness, envy, jealousy, resentment, disappointment, disgust, apprehension, tension and diffidence. Encourage children to spot and collect instances of these emotions from texts they are reading. Again, a classroom display can be a useful teaching tool. Feature in it a selection of fiction and recount extracts, labelled to explain the emotions conveyed in each.

. . . through fiction or recount

Undertake this activity having read fiction, biography, autobiography or other non-fiction text in which the feelings of one or more characters change, and are either described explicitly or can be inferred. Ask children either:

- where feelings are not always clearly stated, to write and stick 'feelings bubbles' (like thought bubbles) beside characters' heads in accompanying illustrations, if there are any; otherwise, beside a series of stick-figure representations of the characters (produced by you or the children in advance); or

- where thoughts *and* feelings are explored or implied, though not always clearly stated, to write and stick 'feelings bubbles' *and* thought bubbles – clearly distinguished, e.g. in different colours – beside characters' heads, whether the characters are illustrated or are stick-figure representations of them.

For example, in Frances Thomas's sophisticated picture book *Mr Bear and the Bear*, children can stick feelings bubbles beside both man and bear throughout the text, speculating on their parallel 'emotional journeys'. Having read a real-life account of a tornado by the daughter in a family, children can draw stick figures representing the girl and her parents and brother at various stages of her recount and give them thought and feelings bubbles. Get sophisticated thinkers about feelings to study texts in which characters deny or hide them, such as Libby Hathorn's *Way Home*.

DIFFERENTIATION

Give emotionally mature children opportunities to investigate texts whose characters are notably unlike themselves: adults, fantastical characters, people from other cultures or times, personalities with problems outside the children's own experience, etc. Encourage them to speculate on these more 'foreign' sets of thoughts and emotions. Also choose texts in which characters' feelings are hidden or unstated, and must be inferred.

With less certain readers, break the read into stages and ask them to record feelings as they occur. Thus when the read is finished, they will still have an overview of the character/s' 'emotional journey'. (Alternatively, ask the unconfident to speculate on characters' emotions only, not on their thoughts as well; to focus on these in one part of the text, or one character, only; or to pool their ideas for thought and feelings bubbles to partners who can scribe for them.)

After any such reading activity, encourage children to share and compare similar experiences and emotions they have known in their own lives.

. . . through metacognition

As in the 'How was it?' activity in the 'Critical thinking' section of this chapter (page 64), prime children to remain aware, throughout a reading task, of:

- how they feel when they first see the text and know they are going to read it;
- in the case of a story, what they think when they encounter the opening of the text, and the first character, setting or event;
- in fiction, how they think differently as they encounter further characters, settings or events;
- in the case of non-fiction, what they think or do when they encounter facts and features they didn't expect;
- whether some aspects of the text remind them of other texts, films, TV programmes, personal experiences, etc. ('intertextuality');
- how they react if faced with vocabulary they don't know, textual links or sentence constructions they find hard; and/or
- whether they feel differently, or are surprised, as they read more.

Give each reader a list of the above aspects and ask them to jot down their responses during or after the reading. Now get them to refine their observations in one of two ways:

- Invite further review: children should now distinguish which of their observations were thoughts and which were feelings; for example they might colour-code their notes into these two categories. (Ensure they are clear about the difference.) Or
- Ask children to review their notes orally, as if wearing *either* a red hat® (for their feelings and their thoughts) *or* a blue hat® (for their *thinking about* their feelings and their thoughts). As an example, suppose children have read 'newspaper articles' from Walker Books' *The Greek News*. Invited to review their impressions, one child might 'wear the red hat'® to report her recorded comment, 'I've written down that I thought the article about the navy was going to be an exciting account because of the title "Sea Dog Tells All", but I was quite disappointed, because it was mainly facts.' She might gloss this, 'donning the blue hat'® to remark, 'Sometimes I don't understand the headings in non-fiction. I should know by now that books like this are really a way of teaching children stuff. There are lots of clues in the design of the page, and skimming and scanning first would have warned me.'

DIFFERENTIATION

Both approaches described above are challenging, the second arguably more so. For children who find it hard, revert to the 'How was it?' approach described on page 64.

Risk-taking

Openly discuss, and value with readers, their ability and willingness to take risks; stress that risk-taking, i.e. trying unfamiliar things, is the only way learners learn. Challenge children sometimes to be 'brave enough' to make a choice or take a risk they would prefer not to. One approach is to designate the occasional reading session as a 'risk day'; alternatively, challenge unconfident children to join a 'risk group' or go to a 'risk area', e.g. a reading corner with this title, to read once every week or fortnight. Some examples of risk-taking in reading are to:

- try a 'shunned' genre or author;
- attempt a text on an unfamiliar subject;
- share a text with a different reading group or partner;
- try to read silently instead of aloud (or vice versa);
- practise a 'performance read'; and
- read to someone younger, e.g. a 'buddy' from another class, or help them with their reading.

DIFFERENTIATION

In a mixed-ability setting, not all the challenges outlined above will suit all readers, whatever their ability. Try them and see!

Boosting independence in 'early finishers'

Sometimes individual readers, or an unsupervised group, complete a reading task both successfully and earlier than expected. Identify any children who do so on a regular basis; encourage them in such situations not to come to you but to choose one from a bank of generic 'follow-on tasks', explained briefly on laminated index cards in a box placed somewhere accessible. Typical tasks can be:

- 'Find another text or book which has something in common with the one you have just read, e.g. same genre, character/s, similar setting/s, layout, design features, subject matter, etc. Consider in what ways it is different and in what ways it is similar.'
- 'Write down (or sticker with Post-it® notes) three words, phrases or ideas you found difficult. Use reference books, dictionaries, etc. to discover more about what they mean.'
- 'Record three favourite facts/phrases/lines/sentences (or sticker them with Post-it® notes). Write down what it is you like about them.'
- 'Think about two or three improvements you think your text should have – in design, layout, contents, events, characters, wording, etc. Write these down if you like.'
- 'Look back at what you have just read. Draw your face with a speech bubble beside the mouth. Write in the bubble advice on how to read the text so as to enjoy it and understand it as much as possible.'
- 'Think about your recent read. How could the teacher use it, or part of it, in a lesson about reading or writing? Give him/her some ideas, in bullet points or diagrams.'

Such approaches will foster 'early finishers' ' independence of action and 'learning stamina' while helping them to think further about their reading.

> ## DIFFERENTIATION
>
> These ideas are suited only to able reader-thinkers who truly have successfully finished a reading task.

Ideas from earlier sections

Outlined in previous sections, the ideas in the following three sub-sections also particularly promote affective thinking and emotional literacy.

Problem-solving

Tracking the intended effects of a text on the reader, such as surprise, sympathy, shock, horror, fear or thoughtfulness, for example by plot profiling, helps children to think about and identify their and others' feelings, especially as readers. Comparing and contrasting characters from fiction, or real-life personalities from biographies, autobiographies, magazine articles and other non-fiction texts is also useful: it highlights the variety of human behaviour, relationships and motivations. Use similar headings to those on the grids on pages 45 and 46 to structure such discussions, or ask children to complete such grids themselves. Aspects of personality to compare and contrast might include:

- behaviour;
- motives (or likely motives) for actions;
- patterns of speech;
- powers of observation;
- relationships;
- emotions;
- lifestyles; and/or
- viewpoints and attitudes, e.g. on controversial subjects.

If you are working with children on self-esteem issues, or the notions of respect and tolerance of others, get them to compare and contrast fictional or real-life characters in texts who illustrate these values (or their opposites). Biographies of Martin Luther King describe personal courage in the face of mass opposition, and the values of human equality and dignity; lives of Joan of Arc demonstrate personal courage and conviction; Raymond Briggs's two characters in *The Man* raise the issues of difference and tolerance; the three family members in Dyan Sheldon's *The Whales' Song* demonstrate that people can have opposing views of the world; and comparing the characters in Gwen Strauss's *The Night Shimmy* with those in other Anthony Browne texts, such as *Gorilla*, raises issues of self-image and self-confidence in an unthreatening way.

Under 'Exploring dilemmas', a variety of formats are suggested in which children can investigate how characters from fiction or non-fiction might resolve their difficulties (pages 51–52). Ensure that children have the chance to make 'real-life transference': to share analogous experiences of their own, and to consider what they did, or would do, in similar situations.

Creative thinking

'Elaborate on . . . the story' (page 53) naturally throws the spotlight on to others' thought processes and feelings. It also promotes empathy – children's ability to see situations, and the world, through others' eyes.

Selected aspects of the 'Creative urges' approach (pages 54–55) allow opportunities for work on self-esteem and self-development. While, or after studying a text, ask children to think of:

- one ambition the text gives them, e.g. to become a footballer, to write a better ending, to see or make the film version, to go to South America themselves . . .

- a character or person mentioned with whom they identify, e.g. a younger child who reminds them of themselves as a baby, a character who behaves as they do when they're angry, an interviewed celebrity who uses a phrase they also use . . .

- a character or person mentioned whom they admire, e.g. for their actions, reputation, courage, looks . . .

Ask the children what it was *precisely* about the text or reading experience that made them feel this. If they keep any kind of reading journal (page 63), they could answer such a question periodically in writing.

As suggested earlier, invite children also to speculate about the responses of someone they know well – a close friend or sibling, perhaps. How might *they* answer such a question? This approach again helps to foster empathy: children's awareness of other points of view.

Critical thinking

As a 'Rating and choosing' activity (see page 59), ask children to identify and rate (for example as first, second and third) texts that they feel represent them most (not just their 'favourites'): for instance, three texts to bury in a time capsule in order to convey their personalities and interests. Inviting children to rate several of their recent 'reading performances' – not just their expressiveness or fluency when reading aloud, but their thoughtfulness and comments about texts – will also boost their self-awareness as well as their awareness that all readers have different tastes, qualities, skills, strengths and weaknesses.

'Polarities' (page 61), and the judging and opinion-giving activities described under 'Evaluations' (page 62), also encourage differing viewpoints, plus the tolerance of those of others.

When using reading journals, as advocated on page 63, ask children to reflect in writing on how they cope with problems when reading; not just 'decoding' and comprehension difficulties, but also:

- being distracted by noise, activity or discomfort;
- encountering widely differing views of the same text;
- reading texts they dislike or would not choose for themselves; and
- problems of concentration or 'reading stamina' when reading long or complex texts.

Finally, requiring a group or pair decision for any of the 'Rating and choosing' activities described on pages 59–60 stimulates the development of children's interpersonal skills: their abilities to listen to and appreciate others' ideas, lead or include other group members, negotiate and, where necessary, compromise. The same is true of any other reading activity in which several children are required to produce a joint or single outcome.

Slotting approaches together

Many of the approaches described under 'Problem-solving', 'Creative thinking' and 'Critical thinking' – and in this section too – can be 'slotted together' to create a block of work, or an in-depth study of one or several texts, if desired. Each phase should take children's thinking about their reading to a new level. This in-depth work will also help them to develop 'learning stamina', one aspect of affective thinking.

Questioning skills

In reading, just as in speaking and listening, get children to practise devising interesting and appropriate questions, using 'question frames' where necessary (see page 34–35). If the questions are in response to their reading, however, be aware of the medium in which you ask children to formulate questions: if they do so verbally, they are implementing speaking and listening skills, but if they do so in writing, the demands on children's writing skills may disadvantage unconfident writers and skew the task towards a writing and away from a reading activity.

Oral formats

The formats outlined in the following sub-section invite oral practice with reading-related questions. Some inevitably duplicate those listed in the Speaking and Listening chapter.

Interviews
Ask children to:

- interview 'amateur writers' (e.g. the school secretary, a governor or a visitor who happens to write – in the widest sense – as part of his/her job);
- interview professional writers, book illustrators, workers on newspapers/magazines or book publishers – in person, on webcam or via video conferencing; and
- question people who read (e.g. peers, other classes, teachers, family), for example in a survey about reading, or while hearing live readings, or for book recommendations/reviews.

Written formats

The formats described in the following two sub-sections allow written attention to reading-related questions.

Collections

Ask children to note down questions they encounter, either:

- from their reading (examples of texts containing questions are given in the 'Questioning skills' section of the chapter on Writing, pages 110 and 112); or
- while watching/listening to real or on-screen interviews with authors, or people in role as characters from stories or poems (hotseating).

Invite analytical thinkers to group the questions they encounter into categories of their choosing; suggest to unsure classifiers a few groupings of your own, e.g. 'open' and more 'closed' questions, or questions to surprise and questions to amuse (see Writing chapter, page 109, for more ideas for categories). The questions can then be displayed, under the children's headings, on the classroom wall. Discuss or vote on which are the 'best', most interesting, most amusing, most unusual, etc.

Written dialogues

Give children opportunities to:

- Follow up on the study of an author, or a visit by a storyteller, author, book illustrator, bookmaker or newspaper/magazine publisher, by writing to or e-mailing them with questions about themselves and their work (there are several websites and publications through which they can be contacted). Or
- Investigate a topic in any subject online by inputting questions to a search engine, or interrogating a specialist website through e-mail to its 'Contact us' address.

DIFFERENTIATION

'What/Which?', 'How?' and 'Why?' questions are more challenging to formulate than, e.g. a 'Where?' or 'Who?' question, so urge confident reader-writers to try these. Suggest they also supplement their 'What/Which?' questions with a noun or noun phrase, e.g. 'What kind of?', 'What size?', 'Which stanza?', and their 'How?' questions with an adverb or adjective, e.g. 'How often?', 'How difficult?', 'How quickly?' The most ambitious can try beginning 'What if?', 'Could you have?', 'Would it be possible/better/difficult to?', 'If . . ., then why/how?'

Any 'question frames', such as these, can be provided on a slip of paper to aid the unsure. Provide able questioners with opportunities, while using the formats above, to sustain their interrogations: encourage them to investigate the answers they receive in more depth, e.g. summarising what they have already learnt from their questioning and then beginning again with a formula such as 'Can you tell me more about that?', 'What does this/do you mean?', 'How does that work/did that happen?', 'But didn't you just say?', etc.

Give the least confident the single prompt words only ('Who?', 'Where?', 'When?', etc.).

Looking for puzzles

This method, adapted from the 'Likes, Dislikes, Patterns and Puzzles' method advocated by Aidan Chambers (Chambers 1993), works with any quality text: fiction, non-fiction or poetry. While and after reading a previously unknown text, ask children to note anything that puzzles them about it. Their 'puzzles' may range from the 'macro' (e.g. incomprehension of the plot, the design and layout of the pages or why an author has repeated a word many times) to the 'micro' (e.g. the meaning of a word, or how to use a particular punctuation mark when reading out loud). Ask readers either to note down their 'puzzles' or to flag them in some way, e.g. with a Post-it® note or highlighter pen.

Afterwards, invite them to share and compare the problems they have identified: whether oral or written, they can express these as questions. Now get children to try to help each other with the answers they know, or interpretations they can suggest, for each 'puzzle'. (If desired, you can select one or two 'puzzles' that feature prominently amongst the group or class, and invite a discussion and debate around these alone.)

> ### DIFFERENTIATION
>
> This works well with mixed-ability groups or pairs, as, when the stage of sharing 'puzzles' is reached, the more perceptive can aid others with problems of comprehension and interpretation.

What could be the question with this answer?

This approach, already described, also extends questioning skills: see the 'Creative thinking' section in this chapter, page 56.

> ### PLAN-DO-REVIEW FORMATS: A CASE STUDY
>
>
>
> This sequence of reading-based lessons with a Year 5 class formed part of a history study of the local town (leading, the next term, into a geography-based local environmental study of traffic and road issues). Our activities addressed a block of literacy objectives connected to locating and using information from a wide variety of media, recording and acknowledging sources and comparing how different sources treated similar topics. The unit of study followed the useful and versatile sequence 'plan-do-review', similar to that promoted by Belle Wallace with her TASC wheel (see Introduction, page 4). The work required the children to problem-solve; it also developed their powers of questioning, and their creative and critical thinking.
>
> #### Differentiated objectives
>
> I made children aware of the intended learning outcomes as the lessons progressed (I also differentiated through the resources used, the tasks given and the ways in which children worked: together, with an adult or separately).

Objectives (planning lessons): All children to be able to suggest as many facts or themes as possible about the history of the local town from around 1880 to 1900 (creative thinking). Some to be able to articulate these for, or record them on to, a large, shared concept map; others to complete a concept map independently of adult help; and some to devise their own mind-maps and complete them (problem analysis and/or creative thinking). Some children to be able to formulate at least two questions about the history of the local town with the help of question frames, others without (questioning skills and problem-solving); the most advanced thinkers to be able to group their questions into categories (problem analysis). Most children to be able to discern the most interesting questions, and those most likely to be answered by research (critical thinking).

Objectives ('doing' phase: lessons and homework): All children to be able to collect written information from one appropriate source in answer to their questions; capable or well-resourced readers/researchers to collect information from at least two *different* kinds of sources. All children to be able to locate and highlight or transcribe key words from their source in answer to at least one question, and to record the details of the source – problem-solving; more adept reader-researchers to be able to do so with several facts from several sources without duplicating their notes (creative thinking: synthesis); some children to be able to devise their own paper format in which to combine these (creative thinking). All children to be able to present their research in some non-written format, e.g. presentation, picture, role-play, model, contributions to the large concept map (problem-solving), with some devising their own format (creative thinking).

Objectives (review): All children to be able to reflect on the research process: what they enjoyed, what they did not, and why; some children to be able to say what they would do differently in future, and/or to evaluate their reading research skills (critical thinking).

First two lessons: planning (problem analysis, creative thinking and questioning skills)

Two weeks before the history topic started, I wrote to children and their parents about it. I asked if they could begin collecting material – photographs, books, leaflets, newspapers, downloaded website information, personal accounts from elderly locals, etc. – about the local environment, past and present.

At our first lesson, introducing the topic, I showed the children an enlarged photograph of the row of shops across the road from the school, taken in 1900, with a horse and cart parked before it. Then I showed a recent picture, with traffic passing in front of it. This stimulated much talk about the differences. I next produced a concept map on the board. In the centre, it said 'Our town then'. I had labelled five branches with headings: transport and roads; industry and trade; buildings; lighting, power and water; families and people. I invited the children to contribute any facts they knew (creative thinking). While the least confident map-makers stayed and worked with me on this, inserting sketches and adding notes themselves where able and willing, other children worked independently in pairs on paper copies of the same, uncompleted, concept map (problem analysis). The results represented their current, pooled knowledge and beliefs (however uninformed) about the local community around 1880–1900 – for example, some children thought there were 'only candles' then (none mentioned gas or electric lighting).

The class was used to mind-mapping, so I had also sent some children – those capable of doing so – to devise their own mind-maps from scratch, labelling branches with *their* sub-headings (further creative thinking; their new ideas included the sub-topics parks and green spaces, leisure and sport, and railways). I allowed them to choose whether to do this independently, or in pairs. We then reassembled. The independent children gave feedback from their own maps; I invited them to add new branches, and items of knowledge, in words and pictures, to the original large, displayed concept map.

This process had so far illuminated what the children *already* knew – or thought they knew. I then invited volunteers to come out and, using a differently coloured pen, to insert a question mark in areas of the large map where they felt they knew little, or to circle existing notes that might be suspect, or to add words or sketches to represent things they would like to know about (problem analysis). To finish this first lesson, I asked the children whether they had enjoyed it; *what* they had or had not enjoyed (an easier question to answer than 'Why?'; and what they had already learnt about our town in past times, from listening to each other (critical thinking and metacognition). I explained that at the next lesson, we would be developing their questioning skills – vital to effective research.

By the next day I had added further details from the children's small maps on to the large classroom map. We looked again at features they had picked out as the areas for further research; indeed, volunteers were able to identify a few more that day, since I had now collated everyone's ideas.

I next did a roll-call of interests. I had a piece of paper listing the children's names and, across the top, the eight sub-topic headings we now had on the map (transport and roads, trade and industry, sport and leisure, etc.). I filled it in by asking each child to nominate a topic they could now research. I urged them to bear in mind any useful connections amongst their close family, family friends and neighbours (e.g. if a child's parent was in the building trade, they might choose the theme of buildings; if a child's family had lived in the area for generations, they could elect 'families and people'): this would enable them to use living people's knowledge and expertise during their research. Otherwise, they could choose their sub-topic on the basis of their own interests, or from their knowledge of the materials (pamphlets, etc.) they had already collected at home.

We now looked at the areas on the concept map where further research was clearly needed. I modelled examples of poor research questions that could lead to one-word or very closed answers, e.g. 'Did our town have fewer people?' (likely answer: just 'Yes'!), or 'What was the main kind of transport on the roads?' (likely answer: simply 'Horse-drawn vehicles' or some such!). In such cases we brainstormed ideas for follow-on questions that could stimulate more in-depth research and provide new, detailed information, e.g. 'If there were fewer people/if not fewer people, how many? What ages and occupations?', or 'What further information is there about horse-drawn vehicles?' This provided us with 'question frames', which I recorded on the board, for example 'If so/not, how/what/when/where/why . . .?' and 'What further information is there about this?' We also discussed the importance of devising questions that were appropriate to the subject, and could probably be researched, as opposed to irrelevant, obscure or 'dead-end' questions, such as 'When was the first house built in our town?' (irrelevant to our period of study), 'Why wasn't tarmac invented then?' (obscure and possibly wrong), or 'What was the largest family to live in one house?' (likely to prove unresearchable). This whole discussion highlighted critical thinking.

The children then gathered into seven groups around tables in the classroom, depending on the sub-topic they had chosen (no one had opted for 'light, power and water', and the groups were of uneven sizes, but this did not matter: I was aiming for a strong commitment to, i.e. an affective connection with, the tasks to follow). Needless to say, most groups represented a mixture of abilities at reading research.

I distributed to everyone a grid with four columns, headed 'My questions', 'The answers', 'More details' and 'Where the information came from'. In the first column, less confident questioners had a list of useful question frames, such as 'What kind . . .?', 'What size/shape/materials/job . . .?', 'How often/many . . .?', 'When/how did . . .?'; I had also inserted the follow-on question: 'What further information is there about this?'. In the last column, I had included further prompts: 'name of publication, author, publisher and page'; 'website address and page'; 'title of leaflet or newspaper'; and 'name of expert'.

I now asked all children to devise at least one question related to their topic, recording this and any follow-on questions in the first and second columns of their grids (thus using questioning skills and problem-solving). Of course, children conferred, and they also frequently consulted the highlighted areas on the large, displayed concept map for ideas for questions. I urged children in the groups intent on researching the same theme to try to avoid duplication by sharing the questions they were thinking of before they wrote them down. I differentiated by challenging more confident questioners to devise at least two questions related to the sub-topic; the most thoughtful of all I invited to ignore my grid handout and to devise their own format for recording both questions, answers and sources (creative thinking)! (One child thus drew a circle divided into segments, writing his questions in one segment. He explained that he would write any answers in the neighbouring segment, plus the source references, but that these were likely to lead to more questions, which he could record in the next segment, followed by further answers and references, and so on round the circle, as his research became ever-more in-depth!)

At the end of the lesson, the children shared and commented constructively on each other's questions. We voted on the most promising from a research point of view, and on the most original (critical thinking).

Next two lessons and homework (problem-solving and creative thinking)
The next day, the children began to bring in the research resources they had collected, including written information from 'experts' outside school whom they knew or had found, e.g. local tourist information staff and elderly neighbours. I modelled alphabetical index searching at the start of each session, reminding children of the meanings of entries in bold and italics, and the especial usefulness of substantial page references such as 'pp. 101–29'. I also modelled the process of anticipating synonyms and other vocabulary related to a research question to facilitate the process of skimming and scanning texts: for example, if a child's question was about products made in factories, I showed how they could scan texts for words such as 'manufactured', 'made', 'produced', 'goods', 'machinery', etc. to locate relevant information. I then demonstrated how the children should confine themselves to 'lifting' from texts only the key words and phrases conveying the information they sought, ignoring 'little words' such as 'the', 'there were', 'also', etc.

The children gathered with their books, downloaded pages from websites, etc. in their seven 'topic areas' in the classroom. I supplemented these with resources that I, too, had collected, from the school library and elsewhere. Some children bartered, exchanging resources that they knew other groups would find useful! Then they began using their alphabetical index skills, skimming and scanning to locate *only information related to their questions*. Less advanced researchers scrutinised one source of information only, e.g. a book or leaflet (which either I or they had identified as useful for their research); I insisted that more adept researchers tried to 'fill out' each answer by finding information from several pages of the same document, and that the most capable used several pages from several different sources, without duplicating detail (synthesis: creative thinking).

Where possible, children underlined key words and phrases in the source material itself; if it was precious printed matter, I issued them with acetate sheets, which they gently secured to the tops of pages with masking tape, using non-permanent markers on these overlays to underline the text below. After about twenty minutes, I asked the children to transcribe the isolated words and phrases they had underlined into the second and third columns of their grids, headed 'The answers' and 'More details'. I then modelled how to record references to sources; the children proceeded to note down their own references under 'Where the information came from' on the grids I had supplied (the children who had devised their own recording methods did the equivalent).

I urged more able researchers to use different colours to underline the answers to their several different questions, i.e. to colour-code the information.

Inevitably, some children had discovered less information than they had hoped. They shared their feelings of satisfaction or otherwise at the end of the lesson, along with some of the most interesting information discovered. They then considered whether they could either flesh out their research further, e.g. by using another resource, or produce a more fruitful question (a discussion involving much critical thinking and metacognition). The lesson the next day followed an identical format. It allowed them to pursue these ideas, as did the continuation of this underlining and note transcription exercise for homework, with resources taken or collected at home. In the end, many children successfully consulted and used more than one resource; all the most adept researchers proved capable of eliminating duplication from their notes, despite consulting multiple sources.

Two more lessons (problem-solving and creative thinking)

After the weekend, all the original research resources were stowed away. I now invited all children, in pairs or individually, to plan a way of communicating to the rest of the class what they had learnt about their sub-topic, as recorded *only* in their grids of notes, or other annotation formats. They had a single lesson in which to prepare. I gave less confident planners a limited number of options for this feedback: a role-play, oral presentation or picture (problem-solving); for more capable planners, the choices were limitless apart from the constraints of time, and materials available in class (creative thinking). Consulting their completed research grids alone, children set to eagerly. By the end of the next lesson we had seen labelled models, captioned pictures, mocked-up Victorian newspapers and mimes explained; we had also heard presentations of facts and figures, role-plays of life in factories, homes and schools, and mock-TV documentaries and information bulletins (using a large cardboard TV frame to add authenticity!).

An added bonus was the opportunity for children in the 'audience' to practise their questioning skills again: I invited them to interrogate each other about what they had found out, how they had worked on their 'final product' and what they would still like to know about their sub-topics.

Review (critical thinking)

In a twenty-minute review session, I asked children to reflect on this block of work. I displayed several questions on the board, and asked them to consider, orally with a partner, or in writing, at least three of them:

- What did you do, in what order, over how many days?
- Which parts of the activity did you enjoy or not? What did you like/dislike precisely?
- What have you learnt about designing good research questions?
- Which sources were better than others, and what made them so?
- What have you learnt about using indexes, skimming and scanning?
- What have you learnt about making notes from books, downloads, leaflets, etc?
- What were you good at, and what less so? How good are you at looking for information in more than one place? What would you do differently next time?
- What types of thinking have you been using: problem-solving, creative thinking, critical thinking, enquiry (questioning)? (I had been using these terms throughout the work, and the children were already familiar with them from other study and tasks.)

I encouraged astute thinkers to consider the last two questions amongst their three or more.

After about ten minutes of reflection, children of all abilities were able to express many insights about the work we had done, their own learning and themselves as learners (critical thinking, including metacognition).

CHAPTER 3

Writing

Problem-solving

Writing – other than writing from dictation, or the pure copying of someone else's text – *is* a kind of problem-solving. It is a process of decision-making at all levels: about which ideas or facts to include; how to organise them; what punctuation and vocabulary to use; and more. The teaching approaches outlined below help to heighten children's awareness that writing is synonymous with problem-solving. They can be applied to most writing tasks.

Sorting ideas

Sorting is an analytical form of problem-solving that also involves creative thinking (thinking widely). The following sections describe several sub-categories of this activity.

Mind-mapping

Before embarking on a piece of factually based writing, for example a notice, recount or report, poems based on observation, or persuasion or discussion, give children the opportunity to mind-map what they know about its subject. If this process is familiar to them, after some teacher modelling they can do it in pairs or individually – ideally on to small whiteboards or using pencils on paper, so that they can make alterations easily. If they are unsure, together, as a whole class or group, draw up one large, displayed map – again on a wipeable board, to facilitate adjustments. The subject should be recorded at the centre, e.g. 'Arguments about animal experiments', or 'The life story of —'. Ask children to brainstorm details about the topic; these should be recorded in clusters at the ends of radiating spokes, each spoke representing a 'sub-category' of the subject and labelled accordingly. (Sub-sub-categories may also suggest themselves, branching off from the initial clusters.) If you are doing the map, invite children to help you with what to write or draw, where to place notations, how to 'cluster' items and label 'spokes' (which is where much decision-making takes place) – even adding the ideas themselves. Use not only words but graphics; record and rehearse together accompanying mimes, actions, jingles, mnemonics or jokes to cater for children with different learning styles (see Figure 3.1). When they are actually writing, stipulate the number of items writers should take from the map: for example, material from at least four 'spokes'.

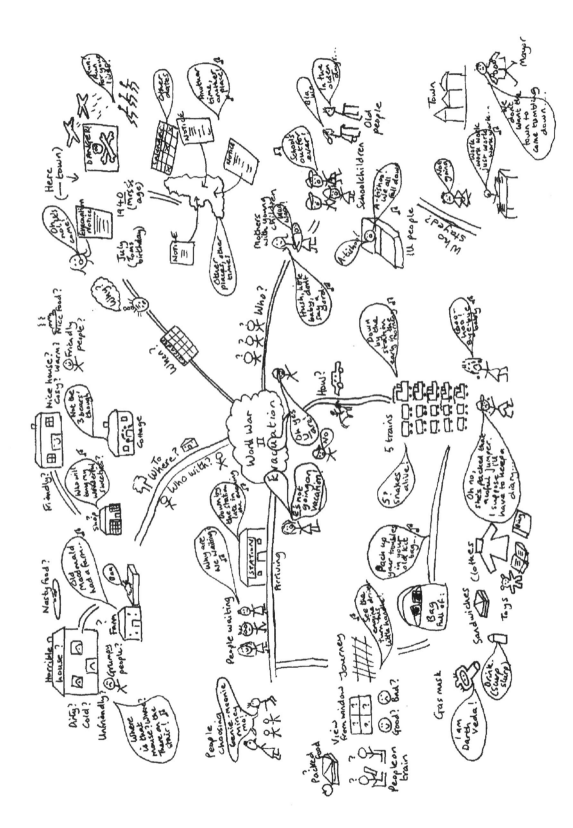

Figure 3.1 Mind-map for a schoolchild's diary of World War II evacuation

Mind-mapping is also useful when embarking on fictional characterisation or scene-setting. Before depicting a character, for example, children might add ideas to spokes labelled with:

- 'Looks, gestures, facial expressions';
- 'Sounds' (of the character's movements, tone of voice, etc.);
- 'Smells' (e.g. perfume, boiled cabbage);
- 'Dress';
- 'Personality';
- 'Relationships with other characters'; and
- 'Home background and past'.

With scene-setting, spokes to complete might include:

- 'Visual details';
- 'Auditory details';
- 'Textures';
- 'Smells';
- 'Weather and light';
- 'Mood of setting'; and
- 'When and where the setting is'.

Children should be free to suggest other spokes. Challenge writers to use one or two items from at least *x* number of spokes.

DIFFERENTIATION

More able thinkers can draw, label and complete their own spokes (as long as they are familiar with the mapping process). It may help to set them a target as to how many spokes, or how many annotations or details, you expect. Use a concept map with the less confident, i.e., supply them with spokes ready-labelled with category headings or 'concepts' (see Figure 3.2). You might even give them one or two items already noted at the end of each 'branch'. It is most supportive of all for an adult to undertake the mapping with a whole class or group.

Mind-mapping also helps children to perceive their learning (in this case, about writing) in context. Together draw up a mind-map to introduce any new writing experience, brainstorming what children already know about the kind of writing required, i.e. differentiating by outcome (for example explanation texts: see Figure 3.3). In this scenario, suggest the labels for each spoke. During the exercise, you are likely to find gaps in children's understanding or recall. Fill these in for them, and draw close attention to these additions as memorably as you can, using sketches, jokes, wordplay, jingles, etc. Clearly annotate or colour-code the areas of your input on the map. It thus becomes a record of children's knowledge so far, for formative assessment – especially if you can save it, for example, on an interactive board or poster.

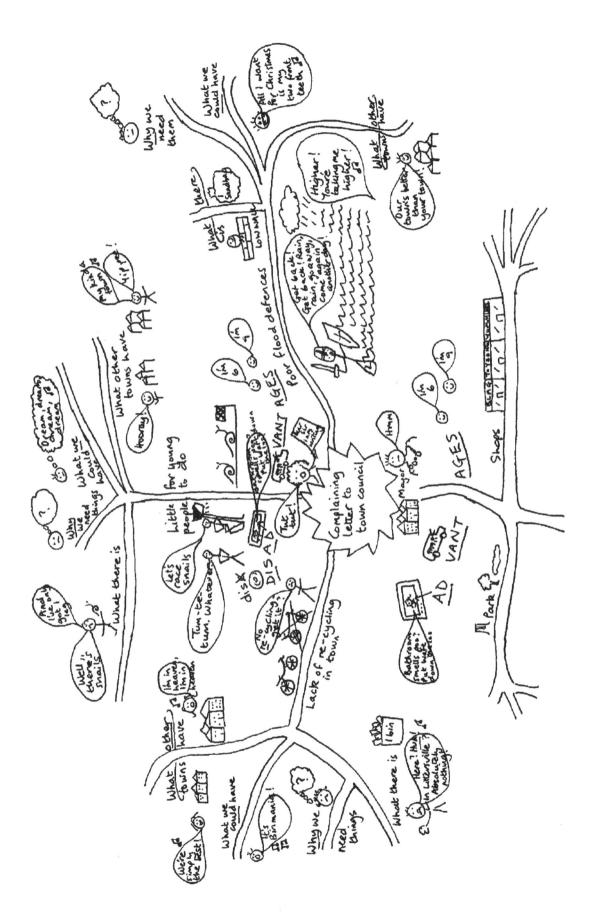

Figure 3.2 Concept map for complaining letter to the town council. The 'advantages branches' could be filled out instead of the 'disadvantages spokes' if children are writing advertising for the town, or both if writing a discussion about its merits and demerits

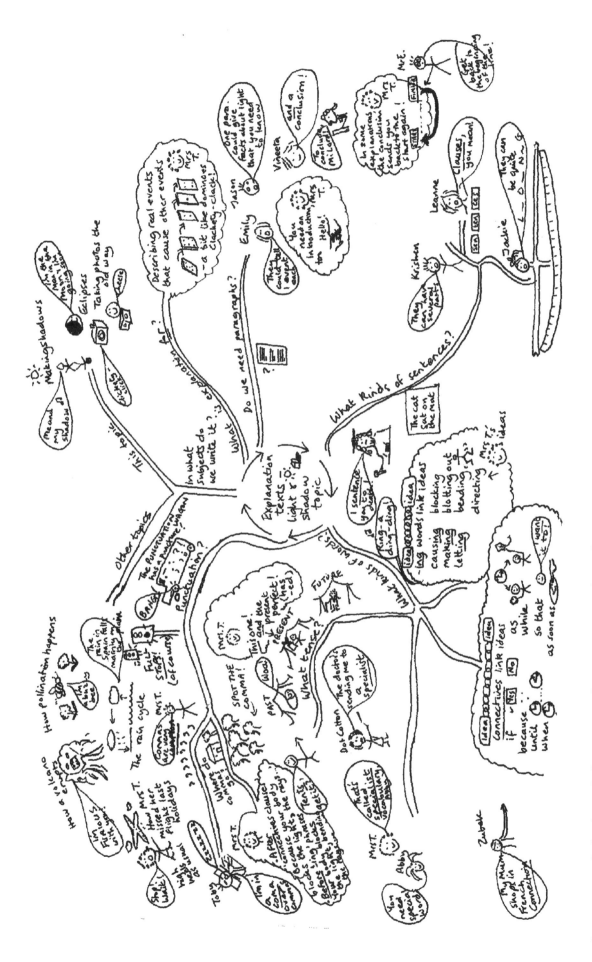

Figure 3.3 Whole-class mind-map on explanation texts, with teacher input

At the end of work on this kind of writing, give children – individually – versions of the same map with the main spokes labelled but no other detail supplied. The children's completion of these will provide information about how much they have learnt.

Sequencing

Sequencing the elements of all written texts presents children with decisions and problems.

● Texts requiring a particular sequence

In chronologically organised texts, for example instructions, recount and explanation, choices about sequencing may be fairly closed but are still essential. (Sequencing becomes a 'puzzle', to be 'solved'.) If children have shared an experience which they are now to 'write up' in some form, ideally provide them with photographs of that experience in its various stages (for instance displayed on a board, or photocopied into multiple sets).

If this is impossible, draw up a grid of boxes, say two rows of four, either on a board or on paper; alternatively, ask the children to do so, or to fold an A3 or A4 sheet of paper into one or two rows of squares (a blank 'storyboard'). Each square should be separated from its neighbour: one method is to cut them up, another to outline them with distinct, not shared, borders. Either ask the children to help you draw sketches, one in each box, in random order, of the main parts or stages of the experience they are to write about, or get them to do this independently (e.g. in pairs or groups). When they have finished, collect examples of what they have remembered from a number of individuals, so that you are pooling your group's recall.

Whether you have provided photographs, photocopies or done sketches, children can then work individually, as a class or in groups to sequence them appropriately, e.g. by numbering them, dragging them into their agreed order on an interactive board or sticking them in a line on to a piece of card. This sequence now provides an aide-memoire to follow while writing.

DIFFERENTIATION

Give children with good recall, and/or writing stamina, more pictures or symbols to sequence. Chronologically organised texts can feature 'detours'. Requiring children to include such 'extras' in their writing will also challenge the adventurous. Once they have established an agreed sequence (as outlined above), ask them to plan into it places where:

● if about to write instructions, they could insert warnings, e.g. safety warnings, or alternative courses of action ('If x happens, do y^1, but if z happens, do y^2'; or 'Now decide whether to do y^1 or y^2);

● if about to write recount, they could add factual background, the reactions of participants, interview quotes or dialogue; or

● if about to write explanation, they could include important facts, e.g. the scientific properties of materials, specific examples of where a process happens or recount of observations or experiments where it happened.

They can indicate insertions by labels and arrows at the relevant points in their storyboard sequence. When confident children proceed to write, ask for several sentences, or even a paragraph, corresponding to each 'box' on their 'board'.

Ensure that children with memory problems are supported by peers with better recall. Also, give them fewer pictures, and/or intersperse the task with discussion and feedback at each completed stage, praising sensible sequencing. When it comes to 'writing up' a text to accompany the storyboard, help the easily confused to stay on task by revealing only one picture at a time (get them to conceal the others in some way, e.g. by turning them face-down, until they are needed).

- Texts with various sequencing options

In texts which are not, or need not be, chronologically organised – for instance stories, report writing, discussions and persuasive text – it can still help to 'storyboard' ideas, by doing sketches and/or notes in each separated box, prior to writing.

DIFFERENTIATION

Insertions, or unusual sequences, are best left to the more adventurous. If confident as writers, encourage children:

- in story planning, to place a box depicting the last dramatic event at the beginning of their sequence; they can then arrange other storyboard boxes to follow on, forming a flashback from this event;

- in story planning, to select a box representing one event to start off their sequence; to follow it with boxes representing any previous events (forming a flashback); and to finish with boxes representing any subsequent events to the first (taking the story forward again);

- in story planning, to add to their chosen sequence two extra boxes, one at the beginning, one at the end, representing some scenario in which characters relate the original story (thus creating a 'story within a story');

- in report planning, to experiment with the order of sub-topics, e.g. for a piece on earthquakes, how they occur, where they occur, spectacular earthquakes through the centuries, and how earthquakes are measured (each represented by a separate box); then, having established a preferred order, to plan insertions, e.g. 'Did you know?' facts and 'Safety precautions' warnings;

- in discussion planning, to shuffle around the arguments for the various points of view (each represented by a separate box), deciding whether to group them by argument, theme or viewpoint, and which sequence of these is most effective; more adventurous children can then plan insertions to illustrate the arguments, e.g. if examining rainforest destruction, alongside conservationists' arguments children could insert futurologists' scenarios for a hundred years' time, and alongside Amazonian Indians' arguments, a description of their future prospects without an income from the rainforest; or

- in planning persuasive writing, to juggle boxes, each representing an argument, to establish whether it is more effective to build up to the most powerful reasons, or to give these first and enforce them with less weighty ones; as above, children may then plan insertions, e.g. scenarios or facts, to back up some arguments.

Pair up or group less confident planners, so that they can work collaboratively. When it comes to writing, help the easily confused to stay on task by revealing only one storyboard box at a time.

Making choices

Giving writers choices highlights the decision-making aspect of writing. The two following sub-sections illustrate this process.

Support for individual writers

Allow all writers *some* scope for choice. Thus if while writing individuals ask you for help, always respond by giving them *options*: two or three ideas for content, alternatives in vocabulary (e.g. a choice of synonyms), options for sentence construction, likely alternatives for a spelling, and so on.

Group approaches

When teaching writing with a class or group, brainstorm options with the children and then record them as a reminder, ideally in words and memory-jogging sketches. For example before children write a story from a given title or opening you might brainstorm ideas for two or three genres that would 'fit' it. Ask children to choose one (suggest that more adventurous writers adapt your examples or choose a suitable genre of their own, i.e. use creative thinking). You can also:

- List a choice of two or three audiences (readers).
- Give children alternative planning methods (notes, sketches, storyboarding, mind-mapping, etc.).
- Show them a choice of layouts (e.g. for a public notice, ranged left, right or centred; for a magazine article, several columns or one, using sub-headings or not).
- Offer two or three sentence constructions, not the simple subject-verb-object formula. These might be *participial phrase*-subject-verb-object, e.g. 'Running out of fuel, people will have to . . .', or *subordinate clause*-subject-verb-object, e.g. 'Because our oil supplies are dwindling, we should think about . . .', or *prepositional phrase*-subject-verb-object, e.g. 'Over the years, it will become harder to . . .'
- Present a choice of voices, e.g. generalised and impersonal ('People', 'Humanity', 'The world') combined with the passive and impersonal ('It is not often realised that . . .', 'This is caused by . . .', etc.), or personal and impassioned ('We must', 'I feel strongly that . . .', 'Have you noticed how . . .?').

> ## DIFFERENTIATION
>
> On the whole, a wider range of choices – or free choice – is particularly challenging for able thinkers and writers.

How can you manage?

Conversely, limiting children's resources or 'writing palette' also presents them with thought-provoking challenges. For writers with a tendency to shapeless length or lack of clarity, it can be a useful discipline, too. For instance:

- Restrict the number of children's story characters to two or three (although, within the genre set, allow writers to choose whose theirs are).
- Stipulate one story setting only, of the writers' choice.
- Limit dialogue in narrative, say to two exchanges of no more than six speeches each, every one of which must either advance the plot or build the characterisation.
- When writing dialogue, restrict children's use of 'said' to, say, three times.
- Ask children to construct a narrative that incorporates a given passage, or that moves to a set ending.
- In fiction, disallow direct character portraits, so that children have to manage characterisation through speech, action and descriptions of feelings alone.
- In fiction or poetry forbid direct description, e.g. adjectives, requiring instead that a sense of place or character emerges through powerful verbs, speech, action or characters' feelings.
- Ask children to limit the length of their texts, e.g. to write a fable in a page, a narrative poem in three stanzas of six lines each, or a summary of a book plot or an explanation in less than fifty words.
- Restrict children's use of 'and', 'but', 'so' and 'then' to, say, three times each.
- In poetry writing, bar use of a letter, e.g. 'e'; in any text bar the central noun or noun phrase, e.g. 'ghost', 'water cycle'.
- Remove spelling aids, encouraging writers to try all spellings as they go.
- Forbid the use of rubbers or erasing fluid, which destroy evidence of progress. Invite children to agree an alternative method for when they make mistakes (e.g. neat crossing-out or brackets, both of which preserve a record of their thoughts).

In all cases, encourage children to think *why* you are imposing these constraints; explain the benefits.

> ## DIFFERENTIATION
>
> In a mixed-ability setting, some of these challenges are more suited to some children than others, whatever their ability. Try them and see!

Challenging problems

There are two ways of making a writing task a 'challenging problem', set out in the sub-sections below.

Challenging for the writer

Some children benefit from the stimulation of an unusual format for writing, that requires extra thought, or a writing task that requires research. Some ideas are:

- a script as if for radio or TV, e.g. an advertisement, play, discussion programme or public service announcement;
- a non-fiction text as a Powerpoint presentation or filmed documentary;
- a story or recount written in the present tense (i.e. in the case of a recount, as if it is an eye-witness documentary);
- imaginary 'out-takes' from a story;
- the script for a fantasy role-play game, e.g. on computer, or a fantasy action story, with choices to be made by the player/reader in the course of events;
- a story, or an episode as if for one, parodying a distinctive writer's style, e.g. Roald Dahl or Enid Blyton (outline the content – something mundane, such as an account of making a cake, or walking across a car park);
- a discussion written as dialogue;
- a report designed (in words and pictures) as a maze, with information to 'collect' along the way;
- a text for a different age or interest group, which therefore requires market research;
- a story, play, poem or report that requires research into fellow pupils from another cultural background; or
- a poem written entirely in questions, or exclamations.

Challenging for the reader

Encourage confident writers to 'make readers work' at their texts. For instance:

- In stories, ask writers to hint at feelings and thoughts without describing them explicitly, e.g. 'He stomped off'; ' "Must we?" she sighed'; 'She shook her head at the scene before her.' Such techniques set 'puzzles' for readers to 'solve'. They can also help produce an effective ambiguous ending.
- When writing poems or notices, invite children to do so without punctuation, obliging readers to construct meanings as they read. (Witty writers may enjoy introducing ambiguities or humour this way, e.g. 'Black coffee smells/Of mornings people smoke in cafés', 'Go/Round Visitors in the Hall'!)
- Suggest that writers address or show awareness of the reader with questions, asides or advice ('If you've never played Five-Fish, this is the game for you', 'Be careful not to . . .', 'Why don't you change your mind and . . .?', or 'This tale is not for the faint-hearted.').
- If writing persuasive or discussion text, writers can challenge readers over their views (maybe even leaving spaces for readers' responses!).

Creative thinking

How many ways can you . . .?

. . . arrange a text?

Ideally, children undertaking this activity should afterwards do the next, outlined below.

Decide on a teaching focus. This could be the organisation of:

- clauses and/or phrases within a complex sentence; or

- sentences within a paragraph (fiction or non-fiction); or

- lines or stanzas within a poem; or

- the paragraphs within a shortish prose text (fiction or non-fiction).

Any of these will heighten children's awareness of the many sequencing choices that can be made when writing, and will highlight the necessary links of logic, connectives, punctuation, etc. that accompany these choices.

Children can work in pairs or groups, or as a class. Provide the texts (clauses, phrases, sentences, lines or paragraphs) jumbled up. These could be on separate slips of paper (for pairs or groups), or on cut-up OHT acetates or displayed on the classroom board (for the whole class). (If you are focusing on clauses/phrases within sentences, ensure you have changed any initial capitals to lower case.) The text should be the same kind as that to be used in the next activity, outlined on page 90 (a recount if a recount, a complaining letter if a complaining letter, etc.).

Ask children to try out as many sequences of the components – clauses/phrases, sentences, lines, stanzas or paragraphs – as they can. They should not merely seek some 'right answer' but investigate what permutations are possible. Most importantly, they should *note any changes needed* for each version (e.g. the addition, movement or deletion of connectives and punctuation). If working in pairs or groups, children can record the possible sequences by writing them down. Alternatively, they can number the components in order, using a different colour for each sequence. If working as a class, invite children out either to arrange and rearrange acetate versions on the OHP screen, marking changes needed with a pen, or – if the classroom board is interactive – to drag the text components into the different possible sequences, annotating them on-screen with any necessary alterations.

If working on clauses/phrases within sentences, you could ask children to use the phrases and clauses within Figure 3.4, or the first two lines of Brian Patten's 'One of the difficulties of writing a poem'. These are: 'On to the he thrust | struggling to his feet | at the beast | which lunged at him | with his sword | with its fearsome teeth and claws |

(a) Struggling to his feet, he thrust with his sword at the beast which lunged at him with its fearsome teeth and claws.

Comments Quite exciting. 'with his sword' sort of interrupts the notion of the thrusting. The beast is frightening so should it be nearer the start of the sentence? The thrusting is important too (he's fighting back). Does it 'get lost' in the middle?

(b) He thrust at the beast with his sword, struggling to his feet. It lunged at him with its fearsome teeth and claws.

Comments It's better with the sword after the thrusting. He probably struggled to his feet before thrusting though, so the first sentence doesn't make sense. Second sentence has more power on its own. You notice it more.

(c) As the beast lunged at him with its fearsome teeth and claws, he struggled to his feet. He thrust with his sword.

Comments Makes it more frightening because you don't know until the second sentence if he is surviving. It's more logical that he gets up before thrusting. 'with its fearsome teeth and claws' sort of interferes with the excitement, though. The second sentence, being short and sharp, is sudden and exciting. Omitted 'at the beast': it's obvious what he's thrusting at.

(d) Baring its fearsome teeth and brandishing its claws, the beast lunged. He struggled to his feet. He thrust with his sword.

Comments Probably the favourite. 'Baring' and 'brandishing' are hard-sounding, alliterative verbs, more exciting than 'with'. Omitted 'at him': it's obvious who the beast is lunging at. Effective short, sharp sentences for the hero. They make you stop and start and keep you on edge about his success.

Figure 3.4   Rearranging phrases and clauses in a sentence

world's shoulders/Snow falls like dandruff'; the whole poem is an exercise in the permutations possible from these lines, and can be revealed at the end!

Give children time to share what different effects they feel are created by different sequences, e.g. changes of emphasis, in priorities, in pace, in what catches the reader's attention most, clarification or obscurity of the sense, or text that reads oddly, etc. Figures 3.5 and 3.6 give examples of sentences or paragraphs to rearrange.

. . . rearrange a text?

Children should now turn to a similar kind of text they have all been writing. Ask them to undertake the same activity on some or all of their own work. (You may flag up relevant sentences, lines or sections, for example with a highlighter, ready for this exercise.) If there has been a time-lag between the above activity and this, find volunteers to share their highlighted writing with the class; transfer a suitable amount of it on to OHTs or the classroom board, and invite other children to help juggle possible sequences (also suggesting any textual changes necessary). This will model the process. Afterwards, ask all children – in ability-matched pairs – to help each other experiment in the same way on their own writing. Make time for feedback. In particular, ask children to share examples they consider definite improvements and unusual permutations.

DIFFERENTIATION

Transposing whole stanzas in poems or paragraphs in prose is arguably the hardest rearrangement, as some sequences are possible only with major editing.

For less secure writers, keep the work on a model text, and that on their own writing, within the same session. Ensure that the text used is manageable in quantity and within children's readability level. Provide a list of connectives that might help them to 'reconnect' transposed sequences. Ensure that someone reads out each permutated version, so that they can hear how it sounds.

. . . disguise your message?

Show children examples of texts that 'disguise' their intentions, for example:

- an information text, recount or newspaper report that aims covertly to persuade (i.e. is biased);
- instructions that also provide information, e.g. about how materials behave in certain conditions; or
- a play that, beside the narrative, presents different points of view on a subject (i.e. is a form of discussion).

Thereafter, while less expert children may be writing a text in its 'pure' form, e.g. making it simply informative, ask those who need a challenge to 'disguise' their text's true purposes. You might get them to write:

- an information text about gambling that imparts a particular opinion of its pitfalls;

In their weird holographic wrappers, Chokko-crunchies even *look* different.

Chokko-crunchies are unlike any other chocolate bar, salty and sweet at once.

If you want to impress with your snack, buy a Chokko-crunchie.

Mmm! Yummy!

Chokko-crunchies give you salty nuts, crispy bits and sweetness – delicious.

Your friends will be so jealous.

Chomped on a new Chokko-crunchie yet?

Figure 3.5   Example of sentences for arranging and rearranging in a paragraph

- a recount of someone's life revealing the author's views on healthy living;
- a newspaper article betraying bias about an incident at a protest march;
- instructions on building a strong, weight-bearing structure that show the writer's background scientific knowledge;
- a play showcasing several different attitudes to a topic, e.g. bullying, recycling, school uniform; or
- a poem that, by matter-of-factly describing a homeless person or a piece of litter, influences the reader on this issue.

DIFFERENTIATION

This approach is best suited to more perceptive reader-writers.

Do the unexpected

While all children in a class or group are writing, encourage those who need a challenge to 'surprise you', for example:

- to use 'sentences' without verbs (e.g. 'Rain. Heavy rain.' 'A longer school day: a good idea?');

Mrs Sorenson, the captain's wife, brunette, 43, said yesterday, 'I'm beside myself with worry. All us wives and girlfriends have heard nothing from our loved ones. Jim always lets me know if he's held up.'

Captain Jim Sorenson, 48 with two daughters, 9 and 13, has a reputation as an experienced skipper. Two men on board were long-serving crew. The third, Tom Sanders, 17, is new to the Danport area. His parents were too upset to comment earlier today.

On Thursday 14 May the Marilyn apparently left Danport Harbour as normal on a routine fishing voyage. It was all set to net cod and whiting off the Danshire Coast. The boat was last seen on Friday 15th, eight miles out.

The Marilyn suffered damage in storms last autumn. It was subsequently repaired by Lies & Slanders Shipyards. It had recently undergone sea-worthiness checks. A spokesman for L & S claims it passed them with flying colours.

The local trawler the Marilyn has mysteriously disappeared off the Danshire Coast with a full crew of captain and three men. The boat's owners, Fishy Business Ltd of Danport, have refused to comment.

A local weather spokesman has denied rumours of a sudden squall off the coast. 'These have not been confirmed,' he stressed.

Figure 3.6 Paragraphs for rearranging

- to use long sentences or lines in poetry without the punctuation usually needed, for a cumulative or 'breathless' effect, or to make meaning deliberately ambiguous;

- to use deliberate repetition, e.g. 'They ran and they ran and they ran and still they ran', or 'Many people think it's all right to modify crops. They think it's all right not to care what might happen . . .';

- to use slang, jargon, dialect, non-standard English, etc. in dialogue within stories to enhance characterisation;

- in fiction, to portray a seemingly stereotypical character, e.g. a vampire, or a sweet old lady, but to give them one unexpected characteristic; or

- to use an unexpected ending, e.g. a twist in fiction or a warning to the reader in non-fiction.

DIFFERENTIATION

Even risk-averse writers will benefit from such challenges, set periodically, and assessments can be made by differentiation against expected outcomes. However, the examples above will probably need teacher modelling.

Making patterns, making shapes

'Patterns' in texts can be said to occur when an author repeats a device or a feature for effect, for example a word, a phrase, some kind of punctuation, an image, a rhyme or rhythm. 'Shapes' are the patterning of events, or parts or themes of the text. For example at the end of a story a character may return to the setting of the opening, thus making a circular 'shape'; an autobiographer might revert to the theme of his loneliness from time to time, thus creating a 'woven' shape. Patterns and shapes need exploration during reading before embarking on the approaches below.

Some written instances are:

- To repeat a word, phrase or sentence structure, for example during dialogue in a story or play in order to give the reader information about a character; in persuasive or discussion writing to emphasise or dramatise a point; and in poetry, to create a rhythm or to emphasise a sound or image.

- Frequent use of questions or exclamations can create similar effects.

- To use successions of commas in long sentences: in fiction, to build a sense of drama; in explanation writing, to create a sense of continuous 'flow' in a process; and in poetry, to 'pile up' descriptions, possibly in a comic way.

- To alternate short and long sentences: in fiction, in order to surprise the reader or to crank up suspense; in non-fiction, to make the reader pause and reflect.

- To tell parallel accounts, e.g. alternating between two sets of characters in fiction, or ancient Rome and Roman Britain in a recount.

- To repeat and develop a metaphor or simile in the course of a story or poem, e.g. the notion of the sun as a fierce rider, or a ruined house resembling a broken skull.

- To list one set of arguments in discussion writing 'in parallel with', or alternating with, the corresponding counter-arguments.

Language fireworks

Encourage writers to 'show off with' language, for instance:

- To use at least *x* specialist terms connected with a subject, e.g. 'evacuee', 'billeted', 'host family' in a World War II piece (writers can elect which terms to incorporate).

- Before they begin writing, ask them (for example for homework or during ICT) to research language related to the topic/s of the text; e.g. if they are about to continue a story from the point of a plane crash in the desert – the vocabulary of planes, crashes and deserts; if they are about to record a local environmental study – the terminology of traffic, road congestion and pollution. Ask them to compile a glossary. When writing, they should use several researched terms.

- Give children the chance to write non-rhyming nonsense poetry. Give them lists of existing nouns, verbs, adjectives and adverbs all related to the theme, e.g. dancing, or animals. Ask them to experiment with changing the initial, especially consonant, sounds. They can then try stringing them together into 'lines of poetry' between recognisable pronouns, connectives, 'the' and 'a'.

- Give each child or pair a different letter of the alphabet; ask them to design the map of a country all of whose city, town, river, lake, hill, mountain and village names begin with that letter. Each child/pair should then devise the appropriate 'letter section' for an index of those names, alphabetically sorting them according to their second, third and maybe even fourth letters.

Insert . . .

Do this activity while studying a text of any kind. It should have a distinctive style and tone – and possibly, in the case of non-fiction or poetry, a distinctive design or layout too.

Depending on the text type, ask children to write (and possibly design the layout for) one of the following:

- a new paragraph or section for it;
- a new episode for it (in the case of recount or story);
- a new stanza or couplet for it;
- a new pair of letters for it: outward-bound, and the reply;
- a new diary entry for it; or
- a new reference entry or entries for it.

They should imagine that their contribution will be inserted in the middle of the original text (in a position located by you). The challenge for the children is to make the new writing sound as seamless with the original text as possible when read as part of the whole.

DIFFERENTIATION

Allow really adventurous, confident writers free rein on the content; otherwise, brief children on the subject-matter of the new material, as this is not the main challenge. For example, if they are to add a new paragraph to a report text on the planets, you might stipulate that this should give information about newly discovered stars and planets (if not covered in the original text); if they are to add a new stanza to a prayer poem, specify what its theme should be, e.g. terrorism around the world (if not covered in the original poem); if they are to add a new episode to an existing story in which a child is trapped somewhere, you might suggest that in the middle of the drama s/he calls out, and thinks they hear someone answer.

This activity requires children to experiment with the subtleties of the original author/publisher's style, language and, possibly, layout; as such, it may not be suitable for a whole class. Unconfident writers may need to learn more about writing that kind of text from start to finish, using the studied text as their general model.

Transformations

Begin with a shortish text that contains at least some simple sentences, and plain – even unremarkable – word choices. (An anonymised piece of writing from a past pupil can be a useful model.) This should be of a similar type to a text that children have recently written. Display it to the group or class, e.g. on a board, OHP or screen. Invite children to help you edit the text. They should add and substitute words and phrases in order to:

- make the language more specific, e.g. 'poodle' instead of 'dog' in a story, poem or play; 'tree canopy' instead of 'tops of the trees' in an information text;
- make the text more descriptive, e.g. 'scrambled up' instead of 'went up' in a story; 'tiny, jagged crystals' instead of 'crystals' in a scientific explanation; or
- give more information, e.g. 'Emily, *who had only just woken up*, began to scream' in a story; 'Many people do not like eating fresh vegetables and fruit *because they seem to taste bland*' in a discussion text.

Then ask children to turn to the text of a similar type that they have written recently. Invite them to select a few of their own sentences in which they can see that there is room for improvement, and to experiment with transforming them. Working in ability-matched pairs is beneficial, as partners often notice scope for improvement when the original writers do not. Invite readings of sentences in their previous and transformed states; take a class or group vote on the most radically transformed and improved. Note that transformation is not necessarily improvement: ensure there is discussion of when transformation has gone too far, e.g. when it obscures meaning, or makes sentences too long or 'flowery'.

DIFFERENTIATION

Able editors may be confident enough to identify sentences in their own writing that can be improved; others will not. For the latter, before the session mark suitable sentences for work (e.g. with a highlighter). If such activities are unfamiliar or daunting, tackle one bullet point (page 96) per session.

Writing showcase

Once children have completed a unit of work on writing, ask them to design a way of celebrating what they have done or learnt. Some ideas are:

- Advice to others on the writing skills or text type they have used, e.g. in leaflet form (for a leaflet rack in class). Children can consult these when needed on future writing tasks.

- Individual, group or class portfolios of writing. Children can mount selected texts or passages in a large book or folder, and caption them with explanations of what they did and learnt, and how.

- Publication on the Internet, e.g. by sending the writing to a partner school for constructive criticism, entering texts on a children's website, or 'blogging' (consult the Internet for free blogging software).

- Ask children to imagine their text is going to be used for a future lesson on writing. Get them to annotate a copy with key teaching points, and to design a lesson plan around it for the teacher.

Ensure that any intended audience does see, and responds to, the celebrated work.

DIFFERENTIATION

For enthusiastic and imaginative children, it may be appropriate to leave the choice of format open, i.e. offer them the range of options listed above, and even suggest they might have further ideas. For others, it is better to specify one of the bullet-pointed methods. With all writers, ensure they have scope to design the precise details of the format for themselves: this will encourage creative thinking.

Critical thinking

We ask children to review, appraise and seek ways of improving their writing much of the time. The suggestions below highlight these activities.

Reflecting on the process

Before children undertake any writing task, ask them to try to remain alert throughout as to how they are tackling it, in what order, and to their thoughts and feelings. Afterwards, ask some of them:

- to recount what they did, in sequence (e.g. how they planned the task, what resources they used to help them, what choices they made, and what caused them difficulties); and/or

- to show others the features of their writing, using the 'metalanguage' (specialist terminology) of writing as much as possible (e.g. paragraphs, metaphors, complex sentences, colons), for instance by giving a talk or presentation; and/or

- to reflect on how they reacted to the task – what they thought and felt while writing, what helped them with it, and their feelings and impressions when it was done; alternatively

- to record the writing process in some way, e.g. as a labelled flow-chart; and/or

- to jot down their thoughts about it in a writing journal (which might also be a general learning journal). (In this case, you may need to model the process first by demonstrating entries about your personal writing.)

Getting used to 'observing themselves at work' in this way, on a regular basis, heightens children's powers of metacognition.

DIFFERENTIATION

The recording and writing journal methods are particularly suited to more perceptive writers. Able children who still find it hard to keep insightful journals may benefit from 'sentence frames' to support them, e.g. 'I find it difficult to . . .', 'I think I am doing better at . . .', 'I have tried to remember to . . .', 'I am pleased with the way I . . .'.

Children with recall problems should summarise their writing and thought processes orally, *immediately* after they finish writing; alternatively, stop them at several points *during* the task, asking them to outline what they have done and thought so far. Give thinkers who struggle 'closed' questions to answer, whether orally or in their journals; for instance, if they are unsure what they thought while writing, ask them how hard they found it to employ certain techniques (e.g. paragraphing or complex sentence construction), or how they coped if they were unsure what details of the content to include.

Ringing the changes

All developing writers need an awareness of the various phases of the writing process: planning, drafting, revising, proofreading and presentation or 'publishing'. However, beware of demotivating eager writers by giving the impression that, the more they write, the more stages you will give them to complete! The approaches in the following two sub-sections help, sustaining children's interest in their work.

Thoughtful displays

Space out the stages of the writing process on the timetable: for example, undertake a short block of work on planning a text one or more weeks in advance of children's writing it; later, resurrect this planning so that children can write from it. Once they have written (i.e. drafted) a text, leave another week or more before, with your coaching, they try revising or proofreading it; and, if a final 'neat' version is required, for instance word-processed leaflets, leave a further time-lag before they make it. As a result, children will approach each stage with fresh vigour, and more critical eyes.

At the drafting stage, i.e. if the children will later be editing their work, encourage them to write either on alternate lines or on alternate pages, leaving opposite pages blank (asking writers to shade these faintly in pencil will help remind them). This leaves scope for subsequent additions, or re-sequencing of sentences or sections.

At each separate stage of the writing process, before it begins, prepare the children for the fact that one outcome will be a display, explaining, celebrating and appraising their achievement. Thus:

- Mount a wall display (or do an interactive whiteboard presentation) of any materials generated during the planning phase: storyboards, notes, mind or concept maps, word lists, etc. (whether produced by you or the children). Invite the children to caption these. Captions must explain what is important about planning (i.e. that this is when a lot of 'work' in the form of thinking takes place); what each item of planning is; when and why it was done, and by whom; and why it was useful in the planning process. Encourage children to give their opinions (e.g. by voting, or adding comments): which items, notes, storyboard features, etc. are the most original, unusual, detailed, clearest, their favourite?

- At the writing (i.e. pre-corrected, drafting) stage, ask children to label a display of their work to explain what is important about drafting (i.e. that this is where a lot of 'thinking in the raw', including rethinking, takes place) and what the drafting process is (i.e. 'rough' writing, which may be untidy and subject to change). Again, encourage children to give their opinions (by voting or captioning): which pieces of writing show the 'roughness' of the process best, take risks, for example with uncommon vocabulary, or show adventurous changes from the planning stage?

- Showcase in some form the work of editing (i.e. adding to and changing texts, using alternate blank lines or pages where necessary, as suggested above). Divide this phase into two distinct parts: first, revising (making substantive changes, such as sentence order, word choices, splitting text into paragraphs, adding phrases, sentences or more, introducing punctuation for effect, etc.) and second, proofreading (making 'secretarial' changes, such as amending lower-case or capital letters, punctuating for sense and spelling improvements). Ask the children to comment, in captions or labels, on their reasons for the alterations they made, and how they ensured they were clear (e.g. by using arrows, a 'marking code', symbols, neat crossing-out, etc.). Invite the children to vote, or comment in further captions, on changes they particularly like and why; on who in their group have shown particular editorial perceptiveness, or maturity in taking criticism; and on the importance of the messy process of editing (it requires self-critical thinking – a much higher-level skill than neatness!).

- Sometimes highlight the phase of presentation or 'publication' by displaying examples, also captioned. (Remember that this can take various forms, e.g. tape-recorded readings; readings of highly amended, not 'neat', work to an audience; videoed presentations from a script; word-processed text, leaflets or books – it need not be in immaculate handwriting.) Invite children to comment, in their labelling, on the limited 'thinking power' involved in this phase; they can vote on their favourite 'finished products', and justify their choices.

- Finally, occasionally undertake an overarching display of all these phases side by side – ideally illustrating the gestation and production of one writing task. For this, ensure that it is the children who provide an 'overview' of the whole process in headings and/or flow diagrams.

DIFFERENTIATION

An alternative method of display is to prepare a large board with jumbled headings ready for use: 'Planning', 'Drafting', 'Editing', 'Presentation'. Show the children captions that explain each phase, for instance for the heading 'Planning', 'At this stage our thinking can take many forms. We think hard and make decisions but we can change these later if we like.' As a writing task progresses, ask children to match captions to headings; to suggest the sequence for the headings; and to locate where their work should go under the appropriate headings. Ensure that less confident writers are also involved in glossing displayed items with their own opinions and comments: class votes suggested by you (e.g. favourite plan for a story ending, clearest mind-map, most thorough editing job) will help to focus these.

Spot the difference

- Collect and display enlarged illustrations of authors' draft manuscripts, clearly demonstrating the messiness of the editorial process. Illustrated literary diaries and calendars provide a useful source; so too do facsimile editions of writers' texts (held in large public libraries). You may be able to obtain reproduced drafts of Edward Lear's poetry from the British Library in London; Arthur Ransome's work from Georgetown University; Frances Hodgson Burnett's from the Manuscript Division, New York Public Library; or J.R.R. Tolkien's from the Library of Marquette University, Milwaukee, Wisconsin and the

Bodleian Library, Oxford. Incorporate these into your display about the revision stage of writing. Alternatively, show such illustrations to the children side by side with reproductions of the same passages of the authors' published texts (e.g. on an interactive board); invite them to 'spot the differences', for example by highlighting, circling or colour-coding the original words and the changes in the final text. Encourage debate: which authorial changes do the children feel are improvements? Why or why not?

- Over a school year, collect photocopies of your children's writing-in-progress: planning on paper, first or incomplete drafts prior to editing, well-edited and final versions. Anonymise these and bank them in a useful format, e.g. as OHTs or scanned-in files. In subsequent years, use them. Ask children to 'spot the difference' from one such stage of a child's writing task to the next. You might supplement their 'thoughtful displays' with some of these anonymised examples. Alternatively, introduce some as a prelude to work on editing or presentation.

- When children undertake a kind of writing they have done with you or colleagues before, collect together copies of their previous similar task. After they have drafted and polished their current work, give out their earlier pieces and invite them to compare the two. Ask them what they have learnt about undertaking this kind of writing from one experience to the next.

DIFFERENTIATION

Inviting children to 'find at least *x* differences' will help to focus this activity, which in its fullest form is more challenging than 'Thoughtful displays', above. Making 'spot the difference' tasks active and interactive, i.e. by asking children to come out and mark up displayed text, will stimulate kinaesthetic learners. Ask the more articulate *why* they feel a 'difference' (i.e. an amendment) is an improvement or otherwise; ask the less articulate *what* it brings to the original text that is better or worse.

Evaluations

Unlike teacher marking, the two formats described in the following sub-sections share the critical thinking with the learner. Choose one or the other – ideally as a whole-school approach.

Critical friends

Pair children up, if possible, based on their progress as writers, handwriters and spellers. (As much as you can, nominate partners who would not choose each other, avoiding both close friendships and 'difficult' combinations!) It may work to use current pairings, e.g. existing talk or learning partners.

For any task in which there is to be a complete 'writing product', e.g. a plan or an edited text, a list of spellings being learnt or tested or a piece of handwriting practice, ask these pairs to sit together. Designate one in each pair as A, the other B. Immediately after your teaching and the writing, ask pairs to show each other their work. Invite A to show their output to B while reading it aloud and B to make helpful suggestions on how to improve it; then, at a signal from you, all Bs can read their work while As give constructive criticism. Set indicators of success, for instance:

- In the planning stage of writing a discussion text, (a) at least three arguments from at least two points of view, (b) an outline of a sequence in which to present them, and (c) a jotted list of specialist vocabulary. Pairs can judge if each has met these criteria.

- While editing a discussion text, (a) the re-ordering of sentences to make arguments more persuasive, (b) the combining of simple sentences to make more complex ones, and (c) a formalisation of the style, e.g. by use of the passive. Partners can again exchange comments on these aspects.

- During spelling learning and practice, ask partners to test each other, e.g. by dictating sentences containing target words. Alternatively, they can check that each has recorded his/her target spellings several times correctly, for instance in a spelling log.

- In handwriting lessons, critical friends can judge each others' letter formation against any teacher modelling of posture, letter shapes, movements and joins. (In this case, partners should comment *while* the handwriting is being done.)

Ensure that it is not the critical friend but the child whose work it is who undertakes any subsequent 'marking' and amendments. (They can use a different colour where appropriate, thus enabling you to view their progress easily.) Praise children who listen to their partners and act on their advice, and those who are polite and sensitive in their criticism.

Self-evaluation

First, involve the children in a critical appraisal of a displayed writing plan or text, for example an anonymised example of a child's work from a previous year, as suggested earlier. Invite volunteers to help you annotate it with suggested improvements. Always start by revising substantive aspects, improving:

- layout;
- word, sentence or paragraph order;
- tedious repetition of words and phrases;
- clarity, amount of detail, inclusion of examples, etc.;
- appropriacy of vocabulary choices;
- appropriacy of tenses, voices and 'modes'; and
- the use of punctuation, for variety, effect and clarity.

Together, use a different coloured pen or marker to improve each of these. Stop after each kind of change (e.g. word order). Ask writers, independently, to revise their texts in this one aspect (ideally in the same colour as you have), before you move on to demonstrate the next kind.

After this repeated process, examine proofreading changes. Invite volunteers to help you improve the displayed text by amending – again, in different colours:

- capital and lower-case letters;
- punctuation for meaning and accuracy (e.g. accurate placement of commas and full stops);
- the logic of paragraph breaks; and
- spellings.

Breaking down the editorial process into small steps in this way, alternating modelling with opportunities for individuals to make amendments to their own texts, helps children build editorial stamina, transfer their learning and progress effectively.

Whichever method you adopt, after an 'editorial session' ask children to share with you:

- what they found hard or relatively easy about the task of improvement;
- what they liked or disliked about it; and
- what they consider their strengths and weaknesses as editors and critical friends.

This heightens their own self-awareness (metacognition).

DIFFERENTIATION

Of the two, the 'critical friends' approach works best with many Key Stage 2 writers. However, reward all mature self-critics by 'promoting them out' of this approach, allowing them instead to undertake detailed self-evaluation and marking – the second method outlined above. (It may help to give them a prompt sheet of the aspects to address when revising and proofreading, such as those listed.) The more children progress as self-critics, the more they can be encouraged to conflate the two editorial processes, revising and proofreading, undertaking them 'in one go'. They should become increasingly able to 'edit as they write'. Encourage proficient editors to generate their own prompt sheets of editorial reminders. These should list their personal priorities, i.e. those aspects of improvement on which they know they need to work.

Affective thinking and emotional literacy

Finding a writing voice

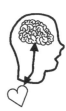

Prior to writing in any genre or text type, ask children to 'warm up' by recording, 'stream-of-consciousness' fashion, their current impressions of their surroundings, feelings and thoughts. (If they are unfamiliar with such an activity, model recording your own sensations first, trying to be as honest as you can, e.g. 'I always get anxious when I have to write in front of the class. When I turn my back, I don't know what's going on behind me, and I feel self-conscious about the children watching me from behind. A door has just creaked open. I wonder who has come in. This pen isn't working very well, but the words are flowing easily so far. My nose is itchy . . .')

The sooner after such an exercise that children turn to their actual writing task, the more likely they are to write spontaneously, in their own 'voice'. Done regularly, this practice fosters their sense of individuality, validating the notion that everyone's writing should seem unique.

DIFFERENTIATION

You may set different criteria for success amongst a mixed-ability group, e.g. length of resultant text (differentiation by outcome), but the activity itself need not be differentiated.

Writing from experience

Rather than embark on story writing by setting a theme, genre or starting-point, invite children to write a recount of something memorable that actually happened to them – preferably recently. Allow them to polish these accounts, using narrative techniques such as scene-setting and well-chosen dialogue. After an interval of a few days, invite them to turn these into stories: perhaps converting the first to the third person, exaggerating some events or episodes, changing names and eliminating unnecessary or uninteresting details. Such an approach often results in unusual levels of commitment from the children, plus a greater sense of authenticity in the finished product.

The same approach can be applied to other kinds of writing. For instance, ask children to write a minutely detailed description of something they saw recently, e.g. in science, before showing them how it can provide the material for a poem; get them to use their notes from an interview with a neighbour or family member to create a biographical or autobiographical piece; or challenge them to write a piece of fiction giving the imaginary background to a topical news story that has struck them.

DIFFERENTIATION

You may differentiate the second phase of the activity in a variety of ways, e.g. working with thesauruses, or a partner, or otherwise, but the first phase – writing from experience – need not be differentiated except, perhaps, by outcome (setting different criteria for success).

Tracking the effects of writing

Whenever children are planning a writing task, ask them to share with you, or with each other, the effect – or effects – they wish to have on the reader. For instance, they may write a persuasive text with the intention to shock and amuse, and to make their readership think differently; a poem in order to move the reader to sadness and sympathy; or a play to stimulate debate about a complex issue, and to provoke moral judgements about some characters. As writers progress, they should become increasingly aware that, in order to be effective, texts should manipulate readers in several ways at different points along their structure.

Suggest that the children devise symbols or a key to represent the various effects they intend in their writing. After they have written a piece, ask them to review their work, for example with a critical friend (see page 101), annotating it in the margins with their 'code' to indicate where each effect is intended: see Figure 3.7. This approach not only allows you and their peers to judge the effectiveness of their output: it also helps to develop an awareness of others' feelings – vital across the curriculum and beyond, not just in writing.

Figure 3.7 Tracking the effects of a story using marginal emoticons (*continued overleaf*)

""Now boy behave, else we'll turn for home," he said in a

soft voice.

They carried on walking and a thick coat of mist

flooded over them like a black blindfold. It started to get

Scared

late but Willow and Ralph had lost all sense of direction and

didn't have a clue where they were going.

"Rrrralph, let's go back ...its starting to get late," Anyway

do you no where we are?" Willow cried ,starting to panic.

Scared

Next thing they knew, there was a sound of cracking

sticks from behind them. Willow and Ralph span round star-

ing... into the distance hedgerows. Ralph grabbed on to Wil-

low ,shaking. The cracking continued. Was someone following

Figure 3.7   *continued*

DIFFERENTIATION

While more emotionally aware children might devise their own symbols or key, you might provide others with a 'bank' of useful emoticons – facial symbols denoting common emotions such as anger, fear, happiness, etc. – and even stipulate which emotional effects you are looking for in children's writing.

Risk-taking

Openly discuss, and value with writers, their ability and willingness to take risks; stress that risk-taking, i.e. trying unfamiliar things, is the only way learners learn. Challenge children sometimes to be 'brave enough' to make a choice or take a risk they would prefer not to. One approach is to designate the occasional writing session as a 'risk day'; alternatively, challenge unconfident children to go to a 'risk group' or 'risk table' to write at least once every week or fortnight. (It may help to have glamorous visual images of risk-taking to hand, e.g. images of young abseilers, potholers, singing wannabees from TV audition programmes, 'hardspelling' competitors, etc.!) Some aspects of writing in which to encourage risk-taking are:

- spelling without aids or help;
- writing (i.e. drafting) without erasers, crossing out neatly instead;
- writing from memory, without pictorial reminders, reference books or planners;
- tackling a blank piece of paper, e.g. writing without the support of 'sentence frames';
- writing 'off the cuff' immediately after a powerful experience, e.g. a field trip, visitor talk or school performance;
- using newly introduced vocabulary, punctuation or sentence structures; and
- writing on a new topic, in a new form or for a new kind of reader.

DIFFERENTIATION

In a mixed-ability setting, different challenges listed above will be suited to different children, of whatever ability. Try them and see!

Boosting independence in 'early finishers'

Sometimes writers complete a task both successfully and earlier than expected. Identify any children who do so on a regular basis; encourage them in such situations not to come to you but to choose one from a bank of generic 'follow-on tasks', explained briefly on laminated index cards in a box somewhere accessible. These tasks should *not* involve 'writing more of the same', or, indeed, a great deal of extra writing, either of which will demotivate children from finishing their work in the first place! Typical tasks (apart from proceeding to edit text with a partner, see page 101) can be:

- Think back over how you started, how you proceeded with and how you finished your writing. Remember how you felt and how your ideas changed. Record this in some way, e.g. in a diagram. Give text references to show the points where your ideas/feelings changed.

- Compare your writing with a similar piece, e.g. a model text used by the teacher or someone else's in your class. Note down three ways in which yours is similar and three ways in which yours is different, e.g. structure; intended reader; style; tone; purpose; tenses used; sentence lengths and structures; use of punctuation.

- Look back over three pieces of recent written work that your teacher has marked. Write back to him/her with your comments. If possible, follow his/her advice and make some improvements to each piece, preferably in a colour so that s/he can see what you have done.

- How would you advise someone else to write as you have just done? List five/ten top tips.

- Imagine someone else could read your mind while you were writing. Draw your face and some think bubbles. In the bubbles, fill in how you have just been thinking as a writer.

- If you could only save three words/phrases/lines/sentences from your writing, which would they be? Mark them in a colour or with an asterisk. Write down your reasons for choosing each one.

- Imagine the teacher is going to use your writing for a lesson. Plan the lesson for him/her, e.g. in bullet points or diagrams. What should s/he say about it?

Encouraging early finishers automatically to pick a card and a further task fosters their independence, while evolving their thinking about their writing.

> ## DIFFERENTIATION
>
> These ideas are suited only to able writers who have genuinely and successfully completed an existing writing task.

Ideas from earlier sections

A number of ideas from earlier sections also foster affective thinking and emotional literacy, as listed in the three sub-sections below.

Problem-solving

During mind-mapping in preparation for writing (see page 79), ensure that children contribute their own suggestions – personal memories, mnemonics, familiar tunes, lyrics and rhymes, factual recall, doodles, etc. – in order to consolidate their learning and understanding. This will boost self-esteem and help make the task personally meaningful.

The 'Making choices' approach (page 86) highlights the uniqueness of every writer in a classroom, encouraging and legitimising children's willingness to 'be different'.

Creative thinking

The more open the choice we give writers – of audience, planning method, text layout, sentence construction, subject matter, etc. – the more creative we are encouraging them to be: it promotes risk-taking and the value of individuality. Asking children 'How many ways can you . . .?' (page 89) encourages them to be flexible and wide-ranging in their thinking – a quality some term 'fluency'.

For children with English as an additional language, invite them to write the imagined words to pictures in their first language, for example a comic strip or graphic novel with the original text obscured. This recognises the importance of their linguistic and/or cultural background and can help build a sense of self-worth.

Critical thinking

'Reflecting on the process' of writing, for instance in a journal (see page 98), can help develop intrapersonal abilities such as self-awareness and metacognitive reflection – as can self-evaluation (see page 102).

On the other hand, 'Critical friendships' between writers, handwriters and spellers (see pages 101–102) can foster interpersonal skills: the sensitive handling of working relationships, mutual trust and respect, and the arts of negotiation and compromise. (Tactful support and constructive criticism are also required in working partnerships during the 'Transformations' approach in the 'Creative thinking' section: see page 96.)

Slotting approaches together

Many of the approaches described under 'Problem-solving', 'Creative thinking' and 'Critical thinking' – and in this section too – can be 'slotted together' to create an extended block of work if desired. Each phase should take children's thinking about their writing to a new level. This in-depth approach will also help them to develop 'learning stamina', one aspect of affective thinking.

Questioning skills

Using texts as models

As children develop their writing, one indicator of its quality is *variety*. This can manifest itself as the use of all four kinds of sentences, of which questions are one (the others being statements, imperatives and exclamations). They should learn not just to write questions in isolation, but to choose them over, or interweave them with, other types of sentence in continuous prose, in order to manipulate the reader. Some texts your children study as models for their writing should contain examples of such interwoven questions, which are classified in the two sub-sections below.

Fiction, plays and poetry
In these texts, some (overlapping) kinds of questions are:

- requests for help, decisions, advice or reassurance;
- requests for information;
- challenges;
- rhetorical, e.g. covert exclamations or 'self-comforters';
- internal monologue;
- dialogue;
- open (a wide range of answers is possible);
- narrow (only one or two answers are possible, e.g. yes/no); and
- closed (the answer is already known, as in rhetorical questions).

Some functions of questions are:

- during dialogue, to give the reader information about character, e.g. mood or personality;
- during dialogue, to reveal relationships to the reader, e.g. who is in control, who mistrusts whom;

- during dialogue, to help move the text along, e.g. to reach a decision or revelation essential to the plot;
- to slow down or even stop the reader;
- to make the reader think; and
- to puzzle or intrigue the reader.

Ask children to investigate these categories through reading first. They can colour-code questions in a passage or passages according to the types and/or functions above. Invite them to share what they have discovered, *immediately prior* to incorporating questioning in any piece of fiction/play/poetry writing that involves characterisation, advancing the plot, mystifying the reader, creating tension or using dialogue. They may or may not base their writing on any structure and patterning in the text just studied.

In fiction, effective texts to study – and possibly use as models – include Susan Gates's *Waiting for Goldie*, Andrew Davies's *Conrad's War*, and many of the fables and traditional tales, e.g. several in Kevin Crossley-Holland's story collection *Short!* In poetry, study, and then write using a framework similar to, Charles Causley's *What has Happened to Lulu?*, *Who's That Up There?*, *Why?* or *Who?*; indeed there are plenty of other poems, many narrative, containing questions, e.g. the anonymous *Meet-on-the-Road*, Jane Whittle's *Dinner Lady* or Sharon Creech's poem-novel, *Love that Dog*. (If your model rhymes, encourage children to use the structure – especially any patterning of questions – *without* any rhyme scheme to inspire their own.)

DIFFERENTIATION

Give confident reader-writers model text containing a variety of kinds of questions, or questions which serve a range of functions. Leave them to establish which categories of question are present in the text. Challenge the most able writers to study colloquial dialogue and questioning through read texts and TV soaps, and formal questioning, for example through historical dramas on TV. Ask them to record and collect examples.

Give unconfident reader-writers model text containing questions of only two or three kinds, or which serve only two or three functions. Tell them which categories (above) they are searching for, and dictate the colour code they should use. If it helps, give them the questions extracted from the text or texts, not embedded within a longer piece (but there should be some text 'around' each question, to make its purpose clear).

When going on to write, specify to stronger writers that they should use *several* kinds or functions of question. In colloquial questions, opening words and phrases are often omitted and left understood (ellipsis). Children should try such forms in their own written dialogue: '[Have you] Ever been/seen/done?', '[Are you] Going out?', '[Is there] No more tea left?', etc. Similarly, challenge them to try formal questions: 'Would you like to?', 'I wonder if you'd mind?', 'Could I possibly?', 'If I may, can I just?'

Tell weaker writers the kinds or functions of questions you wish them to try, e.g. you might ask them to write dialogue in which one character challenges the other in the form of questions showing that they are in a bad mood, or to write a poem in which a repeated question asks for information that is never given, thus intriguing the reader. Unsure writers may benefit from mirroring 'easier' text models such as fiction with a repeated question, a poem with a question as a chorus, a playground chant with a single question or simple variants of it, or a story/play/poem that requires them to devise a question as the title or first line only. If necessary, first brainstorm, or suggest, what that question might be, e.g. 'Who's there?', 'When will it happen?', 'Why are we waiting?', 'What comes next?'

Non-fiction

In non-fiction, the many (overlapping) kinds of questions are similar to those listed under 'Fiction', above. In biography and autobiography, reported interviews, letters and other messages, their functions can be similar too. But in other types of non-fiction their purposes can also be:

- to inform the reader ('Did you know that . . .?', 'Want to know what to do if you lose that round?');

- to make the reader think ('What would happen if you saved all the packaging you'd ever bought?');

- to persuade the reader ('Why don't we all do something now about the dolphins?') or dissuade them ('Are you sure that's the only solution?');

- to worry the reader ('How much longer can the world's population go on . . .?'); and

- to amuse or surprise the reader ('Boys. Why?').

As described above, ask children to categorise and colour-code non-fiction questions in model texts *immediately prior* to challenging them to incorporate similar questions into writing in the same text type, e.g. a non-chronological report, instructions, persuasive letter, brochure or advertisement.

DIFFERENTIATION

Differentiate as suggested on pages 110–111 for fiction, poetry and plays.

Questioning the curriculum

Your announcement of a new topic or unit of work is an opportunity to ask children to write questions related to the subject, informing you of facts or concepts they do not, as yet, know or understand. Giving them a stimulus before they write, e.g. showing work from the last time they visited a similar subject, handling an artefact, looking at related illustrations or playing a relevant sound recording, can help prompt appropriate questions. So, too, can brainstorming or concept-/mind-mapping everything the children *do* know as a class or group. Record and display this list, or their diagrams: these will help the children perceive gaps in their knowledge and understanding. Now encourage them to write relevant queries, reminding them how statements can be reworded as questions, e.g. 'I can't remember when to start a new paragraph' can be converted to 'When do you start a new paragraph?'; 'I don't know where India is' can become 'Where exactly in the world is India?'

Once you have the children's written questions, ask individuals, pairs or the whole class to suggest how to group them into sub-topics, for example for India, climate, farming, living conditions, religion; alternatively, get them to suggest how to display them as a 'hierarchy' – broadest questions at the top to most detailed questions at the bottom, and/or most common at the top to most unusual at the bottom. If possible, present them alongside your planning, displayed in some enlarged, simple format; by cross-referencing to this, point out where you will try to ensure opportunities to answer or explore these questions. Ideally, return to the children's questions (which you can bank) at the end of the block of work. Together, decide which have been answered or explored, and if any remain unresolved. Discuss why that is, and how and when they might be answered.

Bring the work to a close at the end of the unit or topic by inviting each child to record statements beginning 'I would still like to know/learn', 'I am still not sure', 'I still don't understand . . .' (They can even write these up as questioning letters or e-mails to an expert or a character connected with the topic, e.g. a mathematician with whom they video conference, Internet pals at a local school who have already studied the subject or an imaginary early explorer of Mexico; if so, ensure that your writers can receive replies, real or concocted!) Aim to convey that learning is a continuous, never-ending process: there is always more to know and understand. (At the same time, find some way for learners to pursue their unanswered questions further if they are keen to, for example via an interest group on the Internet, a lunchtime club or a self-designed project for homework, to be shared later with peers in class.)

DIFFERENTIATION

Challenge really keen and curious writers to devise the most unusual and interesting questions they can, i.e. questions that no one else is likely to think of. Share a number of non-fiction texts full of deep and ingenious questions in order to inspire the most enthusiastic to devise their own, for example Robert Winston's *What Makes Me Me?* and Philip Ardagh's *Why are Castles Castle-Shaped?* and *Did Dinosaurs Snore?* Challenge strong questioners to design questions that begin 'What if?': it will help if they imagine that one component or feature of something studied was suddenly different. Celebrate the most imaginative questions, e.g. in a class vote. Ensure that such children have the opportunity to research or share them outside the classroom, for example on the Internet with an interest group, or with their families over a holiday, and to report later in class on what became of their ideas.

Give unsure writers copies of a limited number of writing frames for their questions, e.g. 'How does/do?', 'What is/was/were?' Ensure they realise that they *do* already have knowledge and understanding via the brainstorming/

mind-mapping exercise above. For instance, on probing them they might recognise that they know a new paragraph starts when there is a change in something – they just might not remember what kinds of change!

PLAN-DO-REVIEW FORMATS: A CASE STUDY

The following unit of work was undertaken by a group of able Year 6 writers withdrawn from literacy lessons once a week, for up to ninety minutes per session, over ten weeks. While others in class were devising time-shifts within stories, exploring one genre in depth, the approach this group developed together deepened their understanding of several genres, and of timeframes within these. Our work followed the useful and versatile 'plan-do-review' sequence, similar to that promoted by Belle Wallace in her TASC problem-solving wheel (see Introduction, page 4). In the course of this activity, children used creative thinking, problem-solving and critical thinking, and engaged affectively with the task, while its highly collaborative nature helped advance their emotional literacy.

Differentiated objectives

I made the children aware of group and individual learning intentions as the activity progressed and changed (see next section).

Intended outcomes (planning sessions): All children to be able to plan a story in note form on to a storyboard while: selecting several possible effects on the reader (creative thinking); ensuring plausibility, motivation of characters and the fitness of the story's elements to the genre (problem-solving, emotional literacy and critical thinking); and giving enough sense of detail and proportion to enable them to write a well-balanced text, and to guide other writers through their own planning (problem-solving).

Intended outcomes (writing-reviewing sessions): All children to be able to write in a style appropriate to their genre and to sustain a selected narrative viewpoint (problem-solving); all children to be able to adapt willingly and enthusiastically to different tasks and kinds of writing (affective thinking); different children to address their various areas of weakness in writing; all children to help others address their areas of weakness and to brief each other sensitively on their writing tasks (critical thinking and emotional literacy); and all to be able to reflect insightfully in a writing journal on what they were learning (critical thinking: metacognition).

Lessons one and two: planning

My original notion for this work was to allocate a different genre of story to each writer: science fiction, modern realism, historical fiction, detective story, fantasy, traditional tale, myth and mystery story. In addition, I had intended to ascribe a different narrative viewpoint, or viewpoints, for each: a story by a narrator omniscient about characters' thoughts and feelings; a formal report by a narrator uninterested in thoughts and feelings; informal narration of feelings by hearsay; first-person narration by two alternating protagonists; narration by several characters; third-person narration with knowledge of only the main character's feelings; first-person narration by one character; and a story by a narrator who could only speculate about characters' thoughts and feelings.

However, when they heard my scheme the group had more adventurous, challenging ideas. They suggested we put genre options, then viewpoint options, into a box. The children would select from these randomly; then, after the planning stage – to minimise any disappointment from these random allocations – they could write parts of each others' stories in rotation, as in 'Consequences'! After initial horror at the logistical nightmare their proposals presented, I had to recognise and praise the creativity of their thinking. We talked briefly but explicitly about the importance of variety and choice within the creative thinking process; we also talked about the importance of a willingness in life to adapt and try new things; I stressed that their enthusiasm, and the fact this proposal had come from them, were key ingredients in successful learning (affective thinking).

Each child duly picked one genre and viewpoint from a box. Using these they set about planning their stories on to a storyboard (deliberately crudely drawn with headings, to encourage quick notes and revisions: see Figures 3.8a and b). The children were familiar with the format, and happy to annotate, although most others in their class preferred sketching, or planning orally from the headings given.

Planning continued into the next session, as it was crucial to have solid, genre-specific plans, with enough detail to support the 'ghost writers' as well as the planners. I emphasised the need for several effects in their stories, not just one (e.g. to frighten *and* to mystify); for logical motivation of their characters; for plausible events; and for all elements of their planning, e.g. names of characters and details of settings, to 'fit' their particular genres (e.g. Bethany was not a 'traditional tale' name: Margaret, or even 'the woman', unnamed, might be more apt). Depending on individuals, stories would happen within different timeframes, some occurring over hours or days, some over years (creative thinking), thus presenting further challenges.

The children rehearsed their planning, as it evolved, out loud to the group. We all commented, questioning plausibility and motivation rigorously (e.g. asking 'But *why* did he go into the wood?' of the traditional tale plan, or '*How* could your world exist with no ups and downs?' of the fantasy story plan) – critical thinking. Finally, the children checked out their plans in detail with a 'critical friend', who put themselves in the position of a ghost writer and tried to anticipate questions they might need answered (critical thinking).

Eight lessons of writing and reviewing

The next week, children began writing the openings of their own planned stories, i.e. the contents of their first 'storyboxes'. Thus they set the style and narrative viewpoint for other writers to follow. There was also time for readings. As we heard them, the children and I generally demanded an increased use of appropriate detail and stylistic devices to cue the reader in to the genre of each story. Such readings enabled the children also to challenge each other on areas for development or improvement, for example an overly flowery use of description and adjectives that needed paring back; the necessity to check long sentences for structure and sense; or the existence of clumsy repetitions (I modelled critical listening and questioning, the children followed my example).

Before the next session each week, I attached queries and suggestions for each writer, on Post-it® notes, to each text. I then insisted on at least ten minutes of editing and polishing at that ensuing lesson; this was followed by 'before and after' readings, with children illustrating the improvements they had now made, before further writing began. This stage, devoted to critical thinking, was key in moving on the children's writing.

Name of planner: Jack

Genre: Modern realism

Effects on the reader: feel sympathetic and worried sometimes

Narrative viewpoint(s): Informal telling a friend by hearsay

Character notes: Kevin becomes a better person and devotes more time to his family.

What happens to the problem/change: Kevin has to shut garage. Hands over garage to enemy. Pretends to wife that it has been closed by council for health & safety reasons. Enemy has people run garage for him.

Characters introduced: Small family of three. Kevin, 36, father of his new-born baby 5 weeks old. Mother Louise suffering from depression.

Kevin – short man with gruff voice.

Louise – Recently got out of jail wrongly convicted.

Settings: Centre of busy London. Small garage with quite a lot of business. Live in a council run house in a small estate. A lot of gangs hang around the estate. Not the safest place.

Second problem/change: Enemy goes away but later returns for all of his money or threatens to send him to jail for a murder he committed 24 years ago. Does he save himself and not go to jail or save his family.

What happens to it: Gives man all of his money and as a result is made to sell his house. The family has to sleep at friends houses.

First problem/change: Old friend comes (should have gone to jail but didn't). Needs lots of money because he's bankrupt. Wants to frighten his ex-friend. Demands garage or he will harm family. Ta-la-la method.

Ending/resolution: As things get very desperate he hears the news that his enemy has died. Begs a friend for money & buys the business back. He buys a small house and tries to forget the whole experience. K tells wife all about it.

Figure 3.8a Jack's story planner for a particular narrative viewpoint

Name of planner: Amelia
Genre: Science fiction
Effects on the reader: grow to love characters to frighten to make anxious and tense

Narrative viewpoint/s:
Two first persons (Sir Xrangallot & Xrangfie)

Character notes: Sir Xrangallot proves himself

What happens to the problem/change:
Sir X. goes into maze but gets pushed out of centre - so he figures out that he has to face out of it to get into it.
He gets the micro-chip, and he gets back to spaceship and arrives at the palace but....

Characters introduced:
Knight - Sir Xrangallot
Sidekick robot armed with lasers - Xrangfie. Can talk.
Sir X. has lots of gadgets. Has done many tasks for the queen. Never has failed. Very loyal to queen.

Second problem/change:
He gets to queen, and puts in Micro-chip. But he puts it in the wrong way. A slow countdown increases the tension.
Creates suspense.

Settings:
Palace, full of history scenes.
Maze - walls of silver, very shiny. Can't see bolts that fixed it together. Maze smells bitter, sharp and sour. Then in the air.
Maze — seeing shiny walls, bolted together
Sound quiet hum
smells sharp smell, strong
Character half-human, half robot.

What happens to it:
He uses all his strength and pulls the micro-chip out. He puts it back in the right way.
The queen freezes for 5 seconds. Then she moves. She ends up alright. She whispers to the guards.

First problem/change:
Knight must find new micro-ship for slot in queens head if she is not to die (in a weak). Micro-chip is guarded by sci-fi gadgets in an invisible maze (on another planet, far away).
Tra-la-la method.

Ending/resolution:
A few days later, it is announced that Sir X is heir to the throne!
Make this part HAPPY!
Explain feelings!

Figure 3.8b Amelia's story planner for a particular narrative viewpoint

It proved impossible for a pupil to ghost-write someone else's story from the plan alone, so – after the initial editorial phase of each session – the planner of a story would pair up with the child about to write the next 'box' of their plan and brief them carefully, reading the text written so far and explaining their ideas (collaborative work that helped develop diplomatic skills, and thus emotional literacy). There was much exchange of partners at this stage, but the children really enjoyed it, questioning each other closely, so that much affective and critical thinking resulted out of the necessity for friendly, helpful collaboration.

Of course there were hiccups in the 'Consequences' format: occasionally children were absent, and writers often completed each 'box' of their plan, or their briefings, at different speeds. However, there was always scope for improvement or polishing while waiting for others to catch up, or for writing entries in their writing journals about what they had learnt so far or needed to improve (critical thinking); and children helped each other 'telescope' two boxes of their plans on their return, if they had been absent (problem-solving). At every stage, I pointed out what kinds of thinking skill the children were practising and developing.

By the end of ten weeks, eight genre-specific stories, with distinctive narrative viewpoints, had been drafted and polished to a high standard (extracts are illustrated in Figures 3.9–3.11). Through their writing journals, the children reflected widely on the task (they were reassured that these journals were private, not for sharing with others or marking). Their private written thoughts covered their learning about matters as diverse as punctuation and creating suspense, and the logistics of organising such lessons successfully to allow for choice, variety and flexibility!

> about a man who was
> ~~blackmailed out of~~ lost his business
> and almost his life. Poor guy.
>
> Did you see that headline in the newspaper? It reminds me
> of what happened to my family when I was a child. I was
> only 5 weeks, I think.
>
> We had just settled in to our new home in Moxborough.
> Life had been tough for mum and dad. They had met
> in that stupid jail up the road. I don't think either of
> them should have been there.
>
> Now, that's hardly old but he
> felt like he'd lost time!
>
> When my dad finally got out he was 36. My mum was 33
> and although getting out of jail was the best thing for
> both of them, they knew life would be tough as they were
> who isn't!
> short of money. Mum said dad was always cheerful and
> ready to give anything a go! But having no money really
> knocked him back! One of his dreams was to have his own
> business. Now, a car garage was not quite what we imagined
> but it was what paid the bills for the council house. Dad
> worked from 6 in the morning to ten at night. No room
> for a social life!
>
> Mum used to cook and clean and do everything she could
> to help dad as she knew how much stress he was
> under.

Figure 3.9 The beginning to Jack's story, written by himself

Xzangie.

I watched my master ~~walking~~ strolling around the palace. He was very pleased and happy. I dont know why. He smiled at me, and I smiled back. We kept on moving, ~~passed~~ past the tall metal colums. The ~~tin~~ walls were vibrating as I jumped ~~along by~~ beside Sir Xzanyallot to keep up with him. As I walked along with him, I ~~studying~~ studied the ceiling. It was covered with a ~~net~~ bronze, silver, and gold mosaic of a great historic battle. —the battle of Future track The sound of ~~his clunking~~ Sir Xzanyallot's ~~heavy~~ robotic leg. was really starting to annoy me. Our planets race was half human, half robot. So that meant alot of clunking, and chinking. And then I heard someone coming. ~~Both~~ A servant ran towards us flustering ~~his~~ her human arm about. She had a ~~very~~ worried look on her face and was almost whispering. "Something ~~terrible~~ terible has happened. Truely awful!"

Figure 3.10 The beginning to Amelia's story, written by herself (first of two characters' points of view)

Jacks Story

Despite the state of the house, we were happy. The buissness was really starting to pick up. Dad had regulars, the local car fanatics, constantly buying ~~the type~~ old tyres. We were starting to get a good rep. Things were going good!

It was a normal day. Dad got his breakfast of toast and a scraping of butter (we were on a budget), and left with his lucky pen knife in his front pocket.

"Bye love!" mom said.

Dad's fist job, ~~replacing a tyre~~ was to replace a tyre, An easy job for any expert. ~~The day went on~~ He reached out for the bolts and so on. The day went on like this. He stopped for lunch, and perched on the dirty bonnet of some old banger he was working on.

"Well well, Kevin, long time no see!" an unexpected voice smirked. ~~He~~ * kicked the car bumper.
"Nice buissness you've got here!"

Dad was truely ~~startled~~ startled. He was back. The only man in the world that could send my Dad down again.
* A dirty black ~~boot~~

Figure 3.11 The third part of Jack's story, written by Amelia (sustaining the informal hearsay third-person style)

Further reading, contacts and resources

Antidote (2004) *The Emotional Literacy Handbook*. London: David Fulton Publishers.

Bage, G. (2004) *Crosslinks: Reading Writing Thinking across the Curriculum* (history and science-based anthologies and teaching and learning materials). Bangor: Mill Publishing.

Bailey, T. (1987) *Instrumental Enrichment and Cross-curricular Bridging: A Handbook of Suggestions*. London: London Borough of Enfield.

Bearne, E. (2002) *Making Progress in Writing*. London: RoutledgeFalmer.

Blagg, N. *et al.* (1988) *Somerset Thinking Skills Course*. Oxford: Blackwell.

Bloom, B. S. (1956) *Taxonomy of Educational Objectives*. Boston, MA: Allyn and Bacon.

de Bono, E. (1970) *Lateral Thinking*. London: BBC Books.

de Bono, E. (1976) *Teaching Thinking*. London: Penguin Books.

de Bono, E. (1992) *Teach your Child to Think*. London: Penguin Books.

de Bono, E. (2000) *Six Thinking Hats*®. London: Penguin Books.

Bowkett, S. (1997) *Imagine That . . .: A Handbook of Creative Learning Activities for the Classroom*. Stafford: Network Educational Press.

Brown, G. and Wragg, E. C. (2001) *Questioning in the Primary School*. London: RoutledgeFalmer.

Burden, R. and Williams, M. (eds.) (1998) *Thinking through the Curriculum*. London: Routledge.

Buzan, T. (2000) *The Mind Map Book*. London: BBC Worldwide Ltd.

Buzan, T. (2002) *How to Mind Map*. London: Thorsons.

Chambers, A. (1993) *Tell Me: Children, Reading and Talk*. Stroud: Thimble Press.

Claxton, G. (1997) *Hare Brain Tortoise Mind: Why Intelligence Increases when you Think Less*. London: Fourth Estate.

Claxton, G. and Lucas, B. (2004) *Be Creative: Essential Steps to Revitalize your Work and Life*. London: BBC Books.

Comets series (packs of reading books, guided reading cards and comprehension and writing packs for more able KS2 readers). Oxford: Ginn Heinemann.

Costello, P. J. M. (2000) *Thinking Skills and Early Childhood Education*. London: David Fulton Publishers.

Craft, A. (2003) *Creativity across the Primary Curriculum: Framing and Developing Practice*. London: Routledge.

Dean, G. (1999) *The National Literacy Strategy: Supporting and Challenging More Able Pupils in the Literacy Hour*. Cambridge: Cambridgeshire School Improvement Programme, Advisory Service.

Dean, G. (2001) *Challenging the More Able Language User, 2nd edition*. London: David Fulton Publishers.

DfEE (2000) *National Literacy and Numeracy Strategies: Guidance on Teaching Able Children.* London: DfEE. Ref: LNGT.

Eyre, D. (1997) *Able Children in Ordinary Schools.* London: David Fulton Publishers.

Eyre, D. and McClure, L. (2001) *Curriculum Provision for the Gifted and Talented in the Primary School: English, Maths, Science and IT.* London: David Fulton Publishers.

Feldhusen, J. F. (2002) 'Creativity: the knowledge base and children'. *High Ability Studies,* 13: 2.

Feldhusen, J. F. (2003) 'Reflections on the development of creative achievement'. *Gifted and Talented International,* 18: 1.

Feuerstein, R. (1980) *Instrumental Enrichment: An Intervention Program for Cognitive Modifiability.* Baltimore, MD: University Park Press.

Fisher, R. (1990) *Teaching Children to Think.* Oxford: Blackwell.

Fisher, R. (1995) *Teaching Children to Learn.* Cheltenham: Stanley Thornes.

Fisher, R. (1996) *Stories for Thinking.* Oxford: Nash Pollock Publishing.

Fisher, R. (1997) *Games for Thinking.* Oxford: Nash Pollock Publishing.

Fisher, R. (1997) *Poems for Thinking.* Oxford: Nash Pollock Publishing.

Fisher, R. (2001) *Values for Thinking.* Oxford: Nash Pollock Publishing.

Fisher, R. (2003) *Teaching Thinking: Philosophical Enquiry in the Classroom, 2nd edition.* London: Continuum.

Gardner, H. (1983) *Frames of Mind.* London: Fontana Press.

Gardner, H. (1993) *Multiple Intelligences: The Theory in Practice.* Oxford: Basic Books.

Gardner, H. (2000) *Intelligence Reframed.* Oxford: Basic Books.

Gardner, H. (2001) *Good Work: When Excellence and Ethics Meet.* Oxford: Basic Books.

Garnett, Sue (2002) *Accelerated Learning in the Literacy Hour* (books for Years 3–6). Corsham: Hopscotch Educational Publishing.

Gilhooey, K. J. (1996) *Thinking, Directed, Undirected and Creative.* London: Academic Press.

Goleman, D. (2004) *Emotional Intelligence, and Working with Emotional Intelligence* (omnibus edition). London: Bloomsbury.

Goodwin, P. (2004) *Literacy through Creativity.* London: David Fulton Publishers.

Green, M. (2002) *English for the More Able 3 (Ages 7–8)* (photocopiable task sheets). Dunstable: Folens Publishers.

Green, M. (2002) *English for the More Able 4 (Ages 8–9)* (photocopiable task sheets). Dunstable: Folens Publishers.

Green, M. (2002) *English for the More Able 5 (Ages 9–10)* (photocopiable task sheets). Dunstable: Folens Publishers.

Green, M. (2002) *English for the More Able 6 (Ages 10–11)* (photocopiable task sheets). Dunstable: Folens Publishers.

Hackman, S. (1998) *Able Children in the Literacy Hour.* Reading: National Centre for Literacy.

Hackman, S. (2004) *Fast Forward Level 3 to Level 4, 2nd edition* (interactive problem-solving literacy activities). London: Hodder and Stoughton.

Hackman, S. (2004) *Fast Forward Level 4 to Level 5, 2nd edition* (interactive problem-solving literacy activities). London: Hodder and Stoughton.

Hackman, S. (2004) *Fast Forward Level 5 to Level 6, 2nd edition* (interactive problem-solving literacy activities). London: Hodder and Stoughton.

Henshaw, C. (2004) *Thinking out of the Box* (a box of thinking-task cards). Cheltenham: Nijen Ltd, tel: 01242 57535.

Henshaw, C. (2004) *Emotional Intelligence out of the box* (a box of thinking-task cards). Cheltenham: Nijen Ltd, tel: 0124257535.

Higgins, S., Baumfield, V. and Leat, D. (eds.) (2001) *Thinking through Primary Teaching*. London: Chris Kington Publishing.

Jeffers, M. and Hancock, T. (2004) *Thinking Skills: A Teacher's Guide*. Corsham: Hopscotch Educational Publishing.

Jones, J. (2004) 'The Emotionally Literate School', paper delivered at Headteachers' Conference, 'Celebrating Innovation and Creativity'. Bournemouth.

Jones, R. and Wyse, D. (2004) *Creativity in the Primary Curriculum*. London: David Fulton Publishers.

Kerry, T. L. (2002) *Mastering Teacher Skills: Questioning and Explaining in the Classroom*. London: Nelson Thornes.

Krathwohl, D., Masia, B. B. and Bloom, B. S. (1965) *Affective Domain: The Classification of Educational Goals (Taxonomy of Educational Objectives)*. Harlow: Longman Schools Division.

Lake, M. and Needham, M. (2000) *Top Ten Thinking Tactics: A Practical Introduction to the Thinking Skills Revolution*. Birmingham: Questions Publishing Co. Ltd.

Leyden, S. (2002) *Supporting the Child of Exceptional Ability, 3rd edition*. London: David Fulton Publishers.

Lipman, M. (1991) *Thinking in Education*. Cambridge: Cambridge University Press.

Literacy Challenges for the More Able: Books 1–4 (aimed at KS2 children). Corsham: Hopscotch Educational Publishing.

Longman Primary, *The Longman Book Project series* (non-fiction texts differentiated into 'tiers' of reading levels within each book, for a span of reading abilities). Harlow: Longman.

Murris, K. n.d. *Storywise: Thinking through Stories*. n.p: Dialogue Works.

National Association of Head Teachers (May 2004) *Emotional Intelligence and Emotional Literacy*, Primary Leadership Paper 12. Haywards Heath: National Association of Head Teachers.

Nolan, V. (ed.) (2000) *Creative Education: Educating a Nation of Innovators*. Stoke Manderville: Synectics Education Initiative.

Palmer, S. (2001) *Skeleton Books for Reading and Writing Non-fiction and Fiction* (*The Persuasion Book, The Report Book, The Discussion Book, The Explanation Book, The Recount Book, The Instruction Book* and *The Short Story Book*; also available for interactive whiteboards). Huthwaite: TTS Ltd.

Primary National Strategy/DfES (2004) 'Planning for gifted and talented children' section in *Excellence and Enjoyment: Learning and Teaching in the Primary Years: Designing Opportunities for Learning*. London: DfES. Ref: 0520–2004 G.

Primary National Strategy/DfES (2004) 'Developing peer and self-assessment', 'Involving children in self-evaluation' and 'Marking partnerships' sections in *Excellence and Enjoyment: Learning and Teaching in the Primary Years: Assessment for Learning*. London: DfES. Ref: 0521–2004 G.

Primary National Strategy/DfES (2004) 'Independent and individual learning contexts' section in *Excellence and Enjoyment: Learning and Teaching in the Primary Years: Classroom Community, Collaborative and Personalised Learning*. London: DfES. Ref: DfES 0522–2004 G.

Primary National Strategy/DfES (2004) 'Enquiry', 'Problem solving', 'Creative thinking', 'Information processing', 'Reasoning', 'Evaluation', 'Self-awareness', 'Managing feelings', 'Empathy' and 'Social skills' sections in *Excellence and Enjoyment: Learning and Teaching in the Primary Years: Learning to Learn: Progression in Key Aspects of Learning*. London: DfES. Ref: DfES 0524–2004 G.

QCA (2001) *Working with Gifted and Talented Children: Key Stages 1 and 2 English and Mathematics* (handbook, booklet of written examples and video). Sudbury: QCA. Refs: QCA/01/801 and 802.

QCA (2004) *Creativity: Find it, Promote it – Promoting Pupils' Creative Thinking and Behaviour across the Curriculum at Key Stages 1, 2 and 3*. Sudbury: QCA.

Rubery, P. (2004) Section on emotional literacy, in *From Lost Learning Opportunities to Drivers of Attainment*. Nottingham: National College for School Leadership.

Sharp, P. (2001) *Nurturing Emotional Literacy*. London: David Fulton Publishers.

Teaching Think!ng Magazine, from Imaginative Minds Ltd/Questions Publishing Company Ltd, Birmingham tel: 0121 666 7878, *www.teachthinking.com*

Wallace, B. (2000) *Teaching the Very Able Child*. London: David Fulton Publishers.

Wallace, B. (2001) *Teaching Thinking Skills Across the Primary Curriculum*. London: David Fulton Publishers.

Wallace, B. (2002) *Teaching Thinking Skills Across the Middle Years*. London: David Fulton Publishers.

Wallace, B., Maker, J., Cave, D. and Chandler, S. (2004) *Thinking Skills and Problem-Solving: An Inclusive Approach*. London: David Fulton Publishers.

Websites

Antidote: Campaign for Emotional Literacy: *www.antidote.org.uk*

BBC's Listen and Write site for 9–11-year-olds' literacy activities and writing: *www.bbc.co.uk/education/listenandwrite*

'Blogging' software, allowing children to 'post' their writing online: *www.blogger.com*

Book reviews from children: *www.kidsreview.org.uk* (access on subscription) and *www.cool-reads.co.uk* (free) for 10–15-year-olds' recommendations

Buzan Centers: *www.mind-map.com/index.htm*

Centre for Applied Emotional Intelligence: *www.emotionalintelligence.co.uk*

Children's authors' website for 9–13-year-olds at: *www.channel4.co.uk/learning/microsites/B/bookbox/authors*

Children's authors' own websites: a selection at: *www.dis.shef.ac.uk/teaching/children-sauthors.htm*

Concept-mapping software (no SMART board needed): SMART Ideas 3.1 at: *www.smart-board.co.uk* and *education@smartboard.co.uk*

DfES guidance on 'gifted and talented' pupils: *www.standards.dfes.gov.uk/excellence/gift*

DfES literacy plans: *www.standards.dfes.gov.uk*

DfES thinking skills guidance: *www.standards.dfes.gov.uk/thinkingskills/guidance/567257?view=get*

Emotional intelligence: Ei (UK) Limited: *www.eiuk.com*

Excellence in Cities website on the 'gifted and talented', accessible even outside Excellence in Cities areas: *www.brookes.ac.uk/go/cpdgifted*

Fisher, R.: website at *www.teachingthinking.net*

'Internet trails': *www.mape.org.uk/activities*

Metacognition and learning how to learn: *www.learntolearn.org* and *www.acceleratedlearning.com*

Mind Manager (licensed software): *www.m-urge.com*; *www.mindmanager.co.uk*

National Academy for Gifted and Talented Youth (NAGTY): *www.warwick.ac.uk/gifted*

National Association for Able Children in Education (NACE): *www.nace.co.uk*

National Curriculum in Action (2004) *Creativity*, at *www.ncaction.org.uk/creativity*

Paths (Promoting Alternative Thinking Strategies: an emotional literacy programme): *www.channing-bete.com/positiveyouth/pages/paths/paths.html* or *http://modelprograms.samhsa.gov.pdfs/factsheets/paths.pdf*

QCA guidance on 'gifted and talented' pupils: *www.nc.uk.net/gt*

QCA optional extension/assessment tasks in English for more able pupils: *www.qca.org.uk/ages3–14/tests_tasks*

Richard Marsden's Museum Mind Map: *www.walsallgfl.org.uk*

School of Emotional Literacy: *www.schoolofemotional-literacy.com*

Stories from children: *www.creativewriting4kids.com* (access on subscription).

The Sustainable Thinking Classrooms programme, working with children in primary schools in Ulster: *www.sustainablethinking-classrooms.qub.ac.uk*

Teaching ideas (by subject, including literacy): *www.teachingideas.uk*

Teaching plans and resources for literacy: *www.literacymatters.com* and *www.hamilton-trust.org.uk*

Visual Mind (licensed software): *www.visual-mind.com/MindMapdownload.htm*

Writing from children: Kids on the Net at *http://kotn.ntu.ac.uk* and *Young Writer* magazine plus website at *www.youngwriter.org*

Please note that the author and publisher cannot guarantee that the above information, in particular about websites, will remain current.

Index

UNIVERSITY OF CHICHESTER